MW00632904

TALES FROM FATHERHOOD

DETERMINATION · FAITH · LOVE · STRENGTH · HOPE · PERSEVERANCE

Arvie Anderson · Darnell Blackburn · Ryan Brand · Lamar Eason · Ed Gowens
Eric Hodge · Bob Hurd · James Lewis · Ryan McMillan · Demias Pegues
Quake Pletcher · Bryant Seaton · Kareem Washington · Kevin White

presented by
STACIA GOWENS

Enhanced DNA Publishing
DenolaBurton@EnhancedDNA1.com
317-537-1438

TALES FROM FATHERHOOD

Copyright © 2022 Stacia Gowens
All rights reserved.

No portion of this publication may be reproduced, stored in any electronic system, or transmitted in any form or by any means without the written permission from the author. Brief quotations may be used in literary reviews.

Cover Created by Alexis Taylor (Onyxlenz@gmail.com)

ISBN-13: 978-1-7369080-4-4
Library of Congress Number: 2022908968

Anthony,

May the lessons
in these pages guide
your experience of
fatherhood.

Jam G
(pg 51)

Anthony
Tales from Fatherhood shares ideas
to help you grow into this wonderful
role
Bob Hurd

Anthony,
Please enjoy this
book & hopefully
it is a blessing

Ed
Gowns

Stacia Gowens et al.

FOREWORD

By

STACIA GOWENS

D o you all remember the popular sitcom, *Martin*? In one episode, Martin comes to believe that he is the father to a son, Marvin, whose mother he had dated years prior. In one hilarious scene, Roscoe (also played by Martin Lawrence) comes to Martin's house and has a conversation with Marvin about who he is. When Marvin shares that he's just found his dad, Roscoe drops a golden nugget of knowledge: "Fathers; they important to a kid." So true, Roscoe, so true!

I must admit, I feel like I lucked out in the father department. Though my parents were divorced when I was a tween, my father has been a constant presence in my life. From taking me to feed the ducks on the most beautiful campus in all the land, Michigan State University, with ice cream from Tasty Twist afterward, to driving to mom's house in his police car and uniform to break up a fight between me and my sister, and even getting me out of a parking ticket or two on campus, my Dad LOVED me! He has all girls: me, my sister Shannon and my stepsister Marisa, and he doted on us like you wouldn't believe. Add to that I had a loving and involved Uncle Chuck, my mom's oldest brother, a Papa who thought I hung the moon, and even got a bonus dad later in life, Bob, who my kids have known as GrandpaBob (no space as they never took a breath when they said his name as babies) for their twenty-four and twenty-two years of life. All of my 'dads' worked hard. Expected, but also gave a lot. Provided for me financially, intellectually, and emotionally. Trained me how to stand up for myself, be the best I could possibly be, love the Lord, and (in my Papa's words), be brief, be brilliant, and BE GONE!

Through the support I've gotten from my dads throughout my life, I managed to marry a man who is alllllll of that and then some! Edward Gowens is a loving, hilarious, supportive, caring, God-fearing dad who has helped me in raising two amazing human beings, poised to make their mark on the world. Ed didn't grow up with his father in his home, and yet is effortlessly (at least he makes it look that way) and easily one of the most amazing fathers I've ever been blessed to witness—which is saying a lot, given the examples I just shared with you.

It was May 28, 2021, and I was in the space between dreaming and waking for the day when the idea came to me. We were visiting our son in Connecticut for Memorial Day weekend, and I don't know, maybe I was just feeling gratitude for what a wonderful dad my husband is, when I thought, "I know A LOT of amazing dads! Like, all of my male friends, they are truly great dads. Someone needs to tell their stories." So often we hear about all the hard work that mothers do, and don't get me wrong, we surely do! I have, however, noticed that it seems moms are more often publicly praised for it than are fathers. And again, the thought popped into my head, "my guy friends are the bomb.com dads. We should write a book about them. I think I'll title it, *Tales from Fatherhood*."

I pulled together the team that I wanted to share their experiences with other dads. Young dads, older dads, middle-aged dads, granddads, dads-to-be. For all of those who need inspiration from time to time—this book is for you! There are girl dads, dads who were raised without their fathers, and those whose dads never missed a game. There are dads with little kids and those with college graduates. Dads who have kids that are married, and dads that have kids, step-kids, and grandkids. Their stories are enlightening and full of guidance for others about how to make it through the tests and trials that fatherhood is sure to dole out. They will share lessons they've learned, questions to ask, and resources to lean on when it feels as if the fatherhood train is going to steamroll right over you.

I have known some of these dads for over thirty years. They are amazing friends and even better fathers, and I cannot wait for you to be blessed by their strength, smarts, perseverance, prayers, humor, and humility. Without further ado: *Tales from Fatherhood*.

TABLE OF CONTENTS

INTRODUCING DARNELL BLACKBURN

D arnell was born and raised in the City of Detroit and attended Cass Technical High School. Upon graduating from Cass Tech, he fulfilled a family dream of being a first-generation college graduate. He attended Michigan State University and received a bachelor of arts degree in Psychology. Darnell also holds a master's degree in Business Administration from the University of Phoenix.

Darnell spent twenty-eight years working in law enforcement, nine years as a police officer, and nineteen years working for the Michigan Commission on Law Enforcement Standards, the regulatory agency for all law enforcement entities in the State of Michigan.

Recently, Darnell committed full-time to running his company PRAT International LLC (www.pratintl.org). A consulting company that specializes in Inspirational Speaking engagements and soft skills training for organizations in Cultural Competency, Verbal De-Escalation, Implicit and Unconscious Bias, Stress Management, Respecting Differences, and various other trainings.

Darnell is most proud of being a husband to his beautiful wife Ronda and the father of six children ranging from ages twenty-eight down to one year old. Dalonté, a manager of a for a fitness chain; Daryl, who obtained a master's degree and is the coordinator of Leadership and Service programs at a university; Kayla, who received a full scholarship to law school and is now entering into her last year; Kaeden, who is a straight- "A" student entering his senior year of high school; Deuce (Darnell II) who is a rambunctious three-year-old; and Kamari, daddy's last baby boy.

FATHERHOOD AND FAITH

Fatherhood

We walked to the corner store (we walked everywhere) and my daddy let me pick out whatever I wanted. Most of the time it was candy, and any kind of candy I asked for, I got. We walked everywhere because he didn't like driving. I'm not sure if it was because of his inexperience as a driver since he was only twenty-one at the time, or if it was because he did not have a license. After all, he was only twenty-one. For whatever reason, it didn't matter, as long as I was with him and he was with me.

After we left the store, he walked me back to my grandmother's house, which was only about seven blocks away. As he dropped me off at my grandma's, he told me he would see me in a few days. I was nervous and excited because in a few days I was starting kindergarten. My excitement overshadowed my nervousness because I would have my daddy walking me to school and at least for as long as he was there, it would be alright.

Well, that day never came (at least, it didn't come the way I had expected), but my daddy never walked me to school. A few days before I started kindergarten, he died from a heroin overdose at the age of twenty-one.

It turns out my father was what would have been referred to in today's terms as a "crack head". Yes, my daddy was "an addict" and a "dope fiend.". To my family, to the world, that's what and who they saw, but to me, I saw my daddy. I saw a man who would give the world to his son. I saw a man who loved his son. I saw a man who protected his son. I saw my daddy.

Paternal Instincts

Growing up without a father, I had to adopt the good fathers that I saw. Fathers from my church, my friends' fathers, and even television fathers. Most of them never knew they were adopted because I never told them. *I just watched.* I watched them go to work. I watched them teach their children. I watched them discipline their children, but most importantly, I watched them love their children. I was also blessed to be raised by two wonderful women, my grandma and my great-grandma. Sure, they couldn't teach me how to be a man, but as my grandma always said, "I can teach you how a man should be." They taught me how a man should be to a woman, to his children, and to all of his family.

Nineteen years later, I became a daddy. Not on purpose, not intentionally, and not at the right time, but it did happen. In May of 1993, I walked across the stage at Michigan State University, but I still had to finish two classes before becoming an official graduate. In August of 1993, a few weeks after I finished my last two classes, my son was born. I was twenty-two years old, I had no job, no clue, no income, and no idea what was to come.

I had always been paternal. My sister had kids at a young age, and my mother had another son when I was twenty years old. I relished the fact that I was an uncle as a teenager and a big brother to a newborn at the age of twenty. I treated them like they were my own.

Fortunately, I did get a job a few months after my son was born. I became a police officer. My girlfriend and I moved in together and a year and a half later at the age of twenty-four, I had another son. A little over three years later at the age of twenty-seven, I had a daughter.

My family was certainly complete. Or was it? One thing was for sure, and that is that it was certainly growing, but maybe not truly complete. Yes, my girlfriend and I both had jobs. Yes, we were financially stable. Yes, our kids were healthy. For me, though, what was missing in this family structure was a wife and a husband.

Until my daughter was born, I was not sure whether I was supposed to be married to my girlfriend. I questioned myself, my mistakes, my misgivings, and my missteps. I had hurt my girlfriend on numerous occasions and in numerous ways, but each time I hurt her, she continued to be there for me. She never turned her back on me, even when I deserved for her to stab me in mine. So, when my daughter was born, I had an epiphany. My girlfriend loved me despite me. My girlfriend had always had my back. Why had I not given us a chance? Why had I not *totally* committed to her as she did me? She deserved a commitment and so did my precious baby girl. After five years of popping out babies and four years of living together, I spontaneously went out, bought an engagement ring, and popped the question. Just as I had spontaneously asked her to marry me, we suddenly got married a few weeks after I proposed. In hindsight, I cringe at my juvenile rationale and reasoning for getting married.

Marriage is Not Always Best

Marriage is not for the faint of heart. It's also not for people to jump in head first just because they put the cart before the horse. Having three kids before I got married didn't mean I had to get married, but after having two boys first it was something about having my daughter that made me feel I had to. I wanted my daughter to grow up with parents who were married. I took my time getting married. We had been together for six years, but I didn't take my time to build a relationship with my wife first. Though we had been together for six years, my wife and I had only been together for three months before she became pregnant with our first son, and we just kept popping out baby after baby every few years.

As you can imagine, based on how, when, and why I proposed and got married, the marriage went just like you thought it would. It was a train wreck! My misdeeds, mistakes, misgivings, and missteps didn't stop; they were magnified. All the while I never stopped being a daddy to my three children. But the misery of our marriage manifested in me pouring myself into my children and moving further away mentally from my wife. I often had an excuse for why I would and could pour my time into our children and not my wife. My excuse was her work schedule. My wife worked retail and her work hours varied from early mornings to mid-days to late afternoons. So, our family events often consisted of me and the kids going to the park, me and the kids going to the movies, me and the kids going to get ice cream. After school, I mostly made dinner and helped with homework. Now, none of this was a problem for me because I love my kids. Losing my father at such a young age left a void, but it also let me know what type of father I would be to my children. I would love my kids as my daddy loved me. I would spend time with my kids like my daddy did for the short time he had with me. I would teach them the lessons that I was deprived of due to his death. I would make sure I did everything in my power to make them the best or even better versions of me. I was a great father because that is where I put my time, my talent, and my energy, but I still struggled as a husband because after that I had little to give to my wife.

My wife and I were coexisting in our depleted space. Sure, to the outside world we made it look good and we made it do what it needed to do, but we were in shambles.

No Control

On July 22, 2000, I was working the day shift from 7 a.m.-3 p.m. as a police officer. My wife (at that time) had to be at work at 11 a.m., so she dropped the kids off with the sitter as she would do on most days when we both had to work. At that time, we had a seven-year-old boy, a five-year-old boy, and a two-year-old girl. The babysitter was a

16

thirty-year-old woman whom we had met several years earlier when she worked for the daycare establishment we used to take our children to when they were younger. She was like family to us. We trusted her and we loved her. She had been watching our kids for a few years and she was pretty much our only help because all our immediate family lived an hour and a half away.

My wife dropped the kids off as planned and she drove to work. At approximately 11:30 a.m. my cell phone rang. I looked at it and I knew it was the telephone number from my wife's job. I thought, "What didn't I leave out for the kids now, or what did I forget to do, or what did I need to pick up before I got the kids from the sitter?"

After answering the phone, I wish that my wife would've asked me one of those simple questions. Instead, I answered the phone to a voice I recognized but to a sound I could not understand. My wife was crying hysterically, so much so that I could not understand a word she was saying. I kept asking what was wrong and finally, one of her co-workers took the phone and gave me the horrible news that the babysitter and my two-year-old daughter had been in a very bad car accident. The co-worker told me that they had taken my daughter to Sparrow Hospital in Lansing Michigan. At the time, I was a police officer working on the campus of Michigan State University which is in East Lansing, Michigan, about a ten-minute drive from the hospital they took my daughter to.

When I hung up the phone from my wife, I called dispatch on my cell phone and told them I had to get to the hospital because my daughter had been in a bad car accident. As I started driving my fully marked police vehicle to Sparrow Hospital, I did not turn on my overhead lights or activate my siren. I could have used my lights and sirens and been justified. But I did not! I did not because once I heard the news of what happened, I instantly went from being a police officer to a DAD. My mind was focused on nothing but the well-being of my daughter. I completely forgot about my superhero car, my superhero

17

cape, and my superhero badge. I was a helpless mere mortal that could do nothing but pray and rely on my God to supply all my needs according to his riches in glory (Phil 4:19). My need had nothing to do with money as most people often equate this scripture to mean. I knew that God was way bigger than money. My need was healing, deliverance, safety, and to be made whole. I did not know what condition my daughter was in, but I knew who did and I knew who could fix it.

When I arrived at the hospital, I ran in through the emergency section and I asked to see my daughter or the babysitter (never mentioning that my daughter was in an accident I only said her name). The staff thought I was there for a prisoner, another accident, or an investigation involving someone I didn't know. They had no idea that I was there because my own daughter had been in a car accident.

The staff took me to the babysitter and when I walked into the room, her foot was suspended in a sling and she was somewhat incoherent. The babysitter kept saying repeatedly, "he hit me, he hit me", referring to the other vehicle that was involved in the accident. Even though I had no idea how my daughter was, my response to her was, "it'll be ok, everything will be alright". See, the reason I knew that, even though I had yet seen my child, was because when I was driving to the hospital, I stopped at every single traffic light and prayed. I was thanking God and making my request known (Phil 4:6).

I left the babysitter and went to the nurse's station to ask about my daughter. They put me in an area near a back room and I can only remember pacing and praying as I waited for them to tell me something regarding my princess. After pacing and praying for only about five minutes (that felt like fifty), they rolled out this tiny little, angelic baby girl on a giant gurney. She looked beautiful.

I looked down at my baby and there wasn't a scratch anywhere on her.

I kissed her and she said, "Da-da" and I said, "Baby I love you," and the world was well.

A couple of hours later, my wife and I were in the hospital room with my daughter and the doctor walked in to give us his diagnosis. The doctor said, "We've done some pretty nasty things to her legs and she's not responding". My question to him was, "What does that mean?"

He then repeated the same statement. I asked him one more time and he said, "Your daughter sustained a concussion from the accident, she broke her pelvis, and she has swelling on her spinal cord." Once again, I asked aggressively, "What does that mean?" He stated, "We don't know if she'll ever walk again."

As a police officer I was trained to control situations. I fixed other people's problems, I navigated dangerous and volatile situations. I helped people when they were in need. When they didn't know who to call, they called 911 and I showed up. Now I had no control; I could only trust God.

Faith is a Verb!

That day my daughter's life changed. That day my life changed. That day my wife's life changed. That day my sons' lives changed. That day my daughter went from running, jumping, hopping, and skipping to being wheelchair-bound. That day Faith *truly* became a verb in my life. On that day, my faith was put to action from the onset of the ordeal to what the future holds for my daughter and my family. Faith truly was and is the substance of what I hoped for and the evidence of what I don't see. (Heb. 11:1).

Shortly after the accident, my wife and I changed jobs, sold our home, and moved back closer to our hometown to be near family to get support with our children. In 2010, my wife and I divorced, but I never divorced my children. I continued to be the daddy that my daddy was to me.

Today I am a husband again and now a father of six children. My twenty-eight-year-old son is a manager at a fitness center. My twenty-six-year-old son is a director for student events at a university. My twenty-three-year-old daughter is a quadruple threat; she's black, she's a female, she has a disability, and she will be completing law school in another year. My sixteen-year-old son is a straight-A student in high school. My two-year-old son (yes, I said two-year-old) is full of energy. My nine-month-old son (yep, I said that too, nine months) is as cute as he can be.

Through this journey, I've learned to truly trust in the Lord with all my heart and lean not to my own understanding (Prov. 3:5). If I had not learned to trust God, there is no way I would have had my own grandbabies (let that one sink in). It's only because I have learned that my children do not belong to me that I could have enough faith to have more children. I recognize my children belong to God and the only way I can make it through fatherhood again is to trust him. I know that he has given me guardianship over my children, but just like I have guardianship over them, he has guardianship over me.

Fatherhood is one of the biggest blessings that God has bestowed on us. He loves us so much he gave us His name and we can call him FATHER. So, as you continue to read the amazing stories of all of these amazing Dads be encouraged, brother, knowing that iron sharpens iron; *we got this*! (Prov. 27:17).

INTRODUCING EDWARD GOWENS

E dward (Ed) Gowens has been married to Stacia Gowens for over twenty-five years and currently lives in the Dallas, Texas area. He was born in Detroit, Michigan but spent his early childhood in Los Angeles and Pickens, South Carolina. He returned to Detroit to attend high school and graduated from Finney High. He is a graduate of Michigan State University in East Lansing, Michigan, and holds a Bachelor of Science degree in Computational Mathematics. Ed has enjoyed a long career in the Information Technology field and has worked in many industries including financial services, airline, and pharmaceutical.

Similar to the Marvel series called *What if...?*, where different alternatives to the lives of the most famous Marvel heroes are presented, Ed's fatherhood experience could have had alternative choices because he did not have the traditional father-son relationship to build on when he became a parent. The concept in the *What if...?* series gives the viewer twists and turns and different alternatives to consider if just *one* slight change occurred to the story of what we already knew. Similarly, fatherhood can be thought of as a series of "what ifs" because life provides plenty of opportunities to make decisions that may provide different alternatives from what we know or what we expect because of how we react.

FATHERHOOD PRESENTS: WHAT IF?...

What If...My Fatherhood origin story

Before becoming a dad, I wrestled with so many of my own fears about what I didn't have and whether my lack of the traditional family construct was going to negatively impact how effective I would be as a father. Plagued by questions like:

What if I don't know what makes a good father?

What if I can't adapt to my child(ren)?

What if they realize that I am not perfect? (Of course, what I didn't know then was that our children don't need us to be; what all children need is love, consistency, and engagement.)

While I didn't feel I knew everything my future kids would need, one thing I did know was that children need to feel and see that their dad will work to keep them safe from harm. That their dad will protect them, and that even in disciplining them, there is a reason and purpose and, most importantly, that their dad loves them unconditionally. When children are older, it's about being dedicated to their goals and desires, and allowing them to grow into who they are as an individual. It's difficult to unintentionally try to live through our kids as we try to push them into what we may have wished we were at their age. Finding the balance of guiding versus pushing them so that our kids do not resent our opinions and begin to tune us out.

I grew up in a non-traditional home, where my father was not present consistently. To some, this could lead to the perception that this scenario would impact what lessons a child could draw on as it relates to fatherhood. In this instance, I feel what I learned is that it's how an individual leverages key male role models or influencers in their life to provide a foundation to build from. Of course, all of us learn differently and sometimes it's tough to decipher what can be a good influence or what advice would get us from point A to point B.

I saw a lot of patience, planning, and being able to make wise decisions when it mattered most. Interestingly enough, I saw that many men would also confer with or gather advice from others who they knew and trusted to provide guidance in areas where they may not have been as strong or informed. The willingness to search out advice seemed key in how many of my family men lived. It feels slightly different today because I think in today's society the presumption is that we are individuals and that there is no need to regularly seek others' thoughts, opinions, and guidance. The culture is now saying that that is a show of weakness, or it makes the person less of a key decisive individual, when in reality we all need to depend and count on others to help us.

Not having the traditional father-child relationship as a guide does not mean new or existing fathers cannot still impact their children's lives. From my experience, I found that intergenerational friendship with other men who may not have been family but played a key role in being supportive, caring, and involved or interested in my well-being was a great connection that allowed me to see that this would not negatively impact my desire to be a father one day.

What If…Fathers Assemble! (i.e. The Avengers)

Fatherhood should not be just about being a man who is strong and knows everything and can make all of the decisions without some type of support system or other key influencers. Fatherhood is about positive traits such as being forgiving, generous, patient, supportive, gentle, considerate, devoted, clear thinking, and fair-minded. Being a father is the balance between being a man and being someone who has to raise a child(ren) and be responsible for them and their well-being as they mature to adulthood.

The trap to avoid for fathers is to remember not to fall into the stereotypes that can sometimes be associated with being a "man" versus being a father. The best men who are fathers are those who can take a more active role in caring for their children and learning the right balance; in other words, juggling the competing demands of family and work. Fathers must be willing to spend key time bonding with their children (and families, if applicable), as there are advantages for the children to have as much time as possible shared between both parents.

Okay, everyone who has had the perfect situation of having both parents, and in particular your biological father in your home during your entire childhood, raise your hand. If this was a question that was posed to me at any point in my childhood, my hand would have stayed down. Fatherhood can be that much more challenging when the traditional family structure isn't in place to provide you with a blueprint to follow when you reach your fatherhood journey. I was the product of an out-of-wedlock relationship between my mom and dad, and with my dad in the military and my mom moving around, I was never afforded the opportunity to get to know him from a traditional father-son perspective. So, when I had my son, the few things I knew about fatherhood were based on what I *didn't* have and the things I felt I missed out on. For those of us who are fathers, the good news is that all is not lost when one doesn't have the steady involvement or influence from your father.

There were many questions for me once I reached "Dad" status. First, I wasn't sure I was ready and as I looked down at my son, I felt a combination of joy and utter terror in thinking that now I am responsible for this little guy. I was going to need to try to build a life for him that would be significantly better than my experience. Secondly, I felt underprepared and overwhelmed at how I could ever provide him (or my next child) the best life possible without severely damaging them for life.

What I started out with was first just remembering what I knew I had to provide and build from there. So, first I had a house so my kid had a roof over their head. <u>Check</u>. Next, could I feed this eating machine and keep them fed? My wife and I both worked, so we had that covered. <u>Check</u>. Would I love this little guy unconditionally and promise to raise him to the best of my ability? <u>Check</u>!

I had so many questions to ponder and worry about that I didn't fully understand that it wasn't about what happened (negatively) in my life, but how I got to where I was. When I reviewed all the major accomplishments and milestones in my life, I concluded that the journey I made as a young man was about being opportunistic and leveraging different relationships and connections that occurred from early childhood to adulthood. As great a foundation for me a solid relationship with my father would have been, I really did have everything I needed in the many role models who supported me and guided me in my life.

On a recent television special, I watched a program about how we sometimes focus on what negatively went wrong in our lives, instead of focusing on that one person (or people) who continued to support us and believe in us no matter the situation. It wasn't about what I didn't have, who wasn't there, or what I didn't know, because through it all, I was exactly where I needed to be. And to top it off, I know I was blessed with the opportunity to impart to my child the resilience that helped me.

Every role model and father figure I was fortunate to have in my life gave me the bits and pieces to make it to adulthood. Each message or lesson I learned was something that took me farther and gave me confidence no matter what others saw in me or what I didn't think I had. I learned valuable lessons, such as hard work will always trump laziness. I learned that being kind and helping people is rewarding in itself, and that helping others who are on their way up are the same people who could potentially pull you up to get you on the next level. Sometimes it was just as important to listen and observe as to talk without knowing what you are talking about. Being respectful and lending a helping hand is not about you but about putting someone else's needs before yours because at times, it's the right thing to do.

As a father, I realized that I had a network and team of people who supported me and provided me consistency even if it wasn't traditional. With my children, I knew I could provide them not only that traditional father-child relationship that I missed out on, but I would also have the opportunity to build a community of others who can support and teach my kids what my values are even if I'm not around. And more importantly, assembling this network meant my kids would be hearing the same message from other important figures in their lives if they were not as influenced by me as they once were.

What If...Controlling the heart and mind (i.e. Vision)

Being a father of today calls for being more active and involved in the raising and development of children than past generations. As fathers, the more we endeavor to gain a clear vision of ourselves, the more we look to cast a vision for our own fatherhood. We all should realize that we have a lot of imperfections but that should not prevent us from shining through to our children. The vision we should provide is that our children have instances of positive influence from us or other male figures involved in their lives.

What we should hope to create with a vision is an environment that will foster our children to not only think about themselves and their immediate family, but also what impact there is outside in their community. When our children are first born, we spend a lot of time caring for them and trying to nurture them with the right amount of food, exercise, and interaction with key family members. Of course, at this point in life, providing a wordy textbook definition or some type of family statement won't be as impactful because they are not fully developed; however, providing meaningful interactions can help with building the foundation.

We can leverage providing regular affirmation (emotional) with our kids which is just as important as what we feed them for nourishment. Even when our children are young, hugging them and telling them out loud that we love them helps to set the stage and to give them the feeling of belonging to something (family) and of being loved.

It can be difficult to articulate what a vision is that we have in our mind because what we envision initially will change over time as our children grow and develop, and as our relationship and role with them adjusts based on their growth and maturity. As an example, a vision should be positive and focus on a family's strength, attitude on finances, the role of spirituality/religion plays in daily life, what brings satisfaction and fulfillment, and how we relate to family and others in our community.

Here are some key points to consider when creating a vision statement:

- The vision should describe what ideal family life would look like and what a person wants their family to be someday.
- The vision should inspire what one hopes to achieve in five, ten, or more years, and what impact and outcome that will mean for a person's family.
- The vision helps one understand how to carry oneself every day and how it contributes towards accomplishing long-term goals.
- The vision statement should be inspiring, yet short and simple enough that one could repeat it from memory (as should your children).

What if...Being the Shield (i.e. Captain America)

One thing that is true for most fathers is that we see ourselves as the protector of the family. We take pride in being strong and standing up to any dangerous situation that allows us to flex our muscles and snarl through our teeth. At times, we may even be willing to invent a perceived danger just to prove to ourselves or those around us that "we got this!" And although there are obviously situations that would call for us to go into beast mode, there is a balance in knowing when to flex and when strength is more about restraint. Being a father will test not only our strength, but it will test our patience, it will challenge our resolve, and it will force us to know when we must step up versus when it is time to walk away or choose a different path. In each of these situations, as a father, we will find your children looking at us and steadily learning from our actions and reactions.

For most of us as fathers, we are taught from an early age that we must protect those we love and that a show of strength in most cases is the best way or preferred way. Protection for most fathers is in direct relationship to our masculinity and when not leveraged properly can escalate the most innocent of situations into a free for all. But the true challenge of being a father is knowing when to be physically strong and when to be more emotionally and mentally intelligent because not every situation calls for He-Man or The Hulk! When we can show our children the right balance or resolve those situations without force, it can provide them situational examples of how to communicate and appropriately act, and in some instances how to de-escalate. In today's world, being a peacemaker has received a bad rap and is looked upon as being wea, but sometimes protection or strength needs to be more focused on restraint.

As I learned early on, sometimes as a father I needed to realize that what I said, how I said it, and how I responded was being observed and soaked in my kids and they would regurgitate that very reaction/response in the most inopportune time. In those situations, I needed to protect them from myself and my inappropriate response and action.

Another aspect of strength can be seen in confidence. Providing our children the opportunity to grow their confidence and to lessen their fear of certain situations can be a way to protect them from making rash or misguided mistakes. When I was just about a teenager, I was jumped on by some neighborhood bullies and it was one of the most frightening situations I had faced. Not only did I get jumped on, but my homeboy who was with me didn't even try to jump in and help! My mother immediately contacted one of her friends who was a martial artist, and he began to train me in self-defense. During the two years I spent with him, I never had to use one of the things I learned because he taught me that confidence and assurance in one's ability are just like having your own shield, and it helped me put aside the fear of being jumped on again. As a father, providing our children with sensible confidence and courage can be an invisible shield that allows them to stand tall in even the most frightful situations. Have you ever noticed that because some kids, no matter their size, upbringing, etc., are confident, it just seems like everything goes their way, everyone gravitates to them, and they are not afraid of anything? Those are the kids who have good support and role models who instilled in them confidence that allowed them to be a better person. Just remember, do not confuse confidence with arrogance or cockiness. Confidence is positive and isn't about hurting someone or being right at the expense of others. Teaching our kids the difference between confidence and arrogance is what matters for having a balanced young man/woman and a kid who is rude and ill-mannered.

What if...Fatherhood Magic (i.e Dr. Strange)

Fatherhood will teach you many things about yourself and about how well you think you have everything under control. Just like in life without kids, you must accept that there is no easy formula, secret decoder ring, or special words or phrases that we as fathers can use to get the most out of our kids. And just for kicks and giggles, what you think works on one kid does not mean that it will necessarily work on your other kids. This isn't to say that there are not some foundational truths that can be used across the board when raising or supporting more than one child, but you have to be prepared for nuisances and when to adjust your course of action as needed.

I know that for me, once my kids were mobile and could walk and talk (or talk back!), I immediately wanted to look for that imaginary "easy" button from Staples so that I could put them down for a nap, get them to eat their vegetables, or just sit still long enough for me to catch my breath. But, to my disappointment, there is no such thing! What I had to continue to tell myself was that there will never be another opportunity to be close to or engage with my child (children) at this point and that if I wanted to build upon who they were, I would have to be engaged as much as I could even if it meant I would not be able to do what I wanted to do. What I found out is that in some stages of the growth of our kids, we have key opportunities to lay the groundwork that will help shape how they view us, how they communicate with us, and how much trust they will develop in us.

A father or male role model can be that individual who has all the answers to any question, can fix any problem, and of course, can take care of all monsters under the bed. There is a window of time during our kid's life where we as fathers have the best chance of being all of those things to our kids and it is priceless when we sync with them and realize we are like magic to them. There is nothing more amazing and rewarding when your kids come to you with a situation or a problem that they swear cannot be solved or fixed and with the snap of your fingers, you take care of it, and now they are on their way. That feeling of accomplishment and satisfaction is about the best magic feeling we as fathers will get from our children. I loved the feeling of being the answer man or the knowledge wizard for all that my kids needed, and I missed it once my kids were at the age of realization that I *really* didn't have special powers, it's just that I had more experience and had made enough mistakes that I finally figured it out.

The point is that we as fathers will change roles and will take on different priorities in our children's lives as they go from infants, toddlers, pre-adolescent, teenagers, and finally young adults. Our focus is to have the understanding that raising and guiding our little ones is a journey with no secret sauce, no magical wand (well, maybe a good switch every now and again), no full-proof plan or magic cape. The answers we all seek in trying to be the best fathers possible is a hodge-podge of missteps, missed opportunities, and mishaps. But getting back up each time, continuing to push on even when we are weary is all about our roles as fathers. As comedian Chris Rock says, fathers don't always get the recognition or attention that mothers get, but occasionally we do get the big piece of chicken!

Endgame

Being a father never ends, as I've been told. But we as fathers are about providing the foundation and setting up the legacy of our families but being present, involved, supportive, and purpose-driven. Remember, there is nothing magical, one size does not fit all, and when in doubt seek others! Below you'll find some of the questions I deal with in my journey as a father that helps to keep me grounded and determined:

1) What are the strengths you bring to Fatherhood?

- Being involved early on with the kids and making sure to take on responsibilities with the child-rearing (change diapers, storytime, baths, all of it)

- Making sure that the kids see other examples of men/fathers (having them involved with Uncles, Grandparents, and close friends)

- Being consistent, communicating, being present at key

moments, having one-on-one interaction

- Having the control of the narrative as the father

2) What were the challenges as you began Fatherhood? What did you find you were deficient in or lacking?

- Winging it in trying to be an effective communicator

- Learning that some of the things I learned needed to be adjusted based on my kids' needs. Also, how social norms could impact my parenting

- Outside factors like TV, social media, parenting styles of other parents, and sometimes living in suburban neighborhoods and its influences

- Differing parenting styles with my spouse because her relationship with her father was totally different from mine with my father

3) Where do you turn when you need advice?

Here are some recommendations to my fellow fathers. "What If" *you:*

1. Leverage a good network of like-minded individuals—you are not in it alone!
2. Were not afraid to attend or take courses via church or offered via work on parenting (use reference materials)
3. Have discussions with kids and always explain why as parents you've made certain decisions
4. Make sure your kids can have their own relationship with your father, even if you didn't. Don't hold a grudge or hold back from them the ability to interact, even if your relationship may not have been ideal. Of course, you know best, so do so within reason, ensuring it doesn't put the child/children in harm's way.

5. Ask your kids about what they think of you and how you parent them. Feedback is important! We get it at work, and we should not be afraid to get it from our children. It could be a hard conversation to hear, but it can also provide a father a way to more impactfully interact with their children.

INTRODUCING ARVIE ANDERSON

Arvie J. Anderson is a father and husband, married to his wife Kelly Copes-Anderson for almost twenty-five years. Arvie resides in Indianapolis, Indiana where he has lived for over twenty years.

Born in Detroit, Michigan, Arvie attended Michigan State University from 1988 through 1993. After graduating with a degree in chemical engineering, Arvie worked as a process engineer in Indiana. In 1995, Arvie attended the University of Michigan Law School, where he attained his JD in 1997. Arvie has been a corporate patent counsel for over twenty years. Currently, Arvie is attaining a certificate from the Harvard Business Analytics program expected in Spring 2022.

Arvie is an executive board member at Noble and the Arc of Indiana. Both organizations are dedicated to improving the lives of people with disabilities.

MY VISION OF A GREAT FATHER: WHATEVER IT TAKES

I was blessed with an excellent example for a father. Arvie Anderson Sr. was married to his wife (my mom) for over fifty years, and within that time he did whatever was necessary to provide for his family. "Whatever it takes" was always a part of his character. My dad was born in a small town in Arkansas called Mariana, outside of Little Rock. He dropped out of school to help out on the family farm. As part of the "great migration" of African Americans north, along with several of his siblings, he came to Detroit, Michigan to escape the lack of opportunity and racism in the south during the 1950s and 1960s.

After meeting my mom and starting a family, my dad performed several types of physically demanding jobs to support himself and our family. Throughout my formative years, my dad was a bricklayer, foundry foreman, handyman, ditchdigger, and whatever job was necessary to provide for the family. He came home every night and was faithful to his family. Whatever it took.

Education was a point of emphasis for his children. At an early age, both my parents instilled an expectation that we would stay in school and graduate from college. In that endeavor he was also successful. My sister obtained bachelor's and master's degrees. I obtained both chemical engineering and law degrees. My parents supported us throughout this time, and I came to value the importance of education to get a strong start in life.

My Journey as a Parent: First Child

In my late twenties, I married my college sweetheart and I set out on a professional and family path of my own. Soon after law school graduation, we had our first child. As a father, just like my father, I was determined to do whatever it took to provide the best opportunities for my son.

Early in my first child's life, health impacted his development. He had repetitive ear infections which affected his hearing, and in turn his speech was delayed in development. It was only through several years of therapy that he overcame these impediments to become a more typical adolescent from a developmental perspective.

As a new father, development delay in a child can be mentally exhausting. Concerns and fears that go through the mind in terms of the challenges a child can face is a poignant experience. Thanks to prayer, faith, and many hours of therapy, my first son progressed; however, the experience left an impression. It was four years between our first and second child, principally, I believe, because of the challenges we all had to overcome. It is with this background that we set out to have our second child.

My Journey as a Parent: Second Child

I had always wanted two boys. I was simply thrilled to learn that I would be a father to one, and only one, additional son. Our second child did not come quite as easily as the first, but after some work, we were successful. A second son was on the way!

Life can be uncertain, but I felt confident. In spite of our earlier experiences with my first son in terms of developmental issues, I was confident that our second child would be healthy and happy. If not, then after he was born, I stood ready to address and overcome any issues.

As it turns out, as you might imagine, the second child experience was very different. He slept through the night at a very early age. We were more experienced parents, so we knew the ropes on activities, daycare, and the best places to do "all things children." Since we were moving up the corporate ladder professionally, we felt we had more resources and knowledge to address any issues that came up. Our older son was firmly on his way in middle school. The Andersons were on the rise! We were probably overconfident… But who wouldn't be? We had two healthy boys, a stable marriage, and we both had successful professional careers, so there was no reason to believe that our future was anything but even rosier. As the saying goes, "Men make plans and God laughs."

As is typical with children on the autistic spectrum, at around two years old, my youngest son experienced significant delays in development. Having experienced this with my older son, we sought various forms of therapy early to address these issues. However, he became more and more withdrawn from the outside world.

It was around this time he became aggressive toward those around him. These were more than just two-year old tantrums. There was biting, scratching, kicking, throwing of objects, and other various forms of physical outbursts. He would perseverate, refusing to move on from a stimulating activity involving movement. Each transition from one activity to the next could be met with an aggressive outburst.

One example of this behavior which comes to mind involved the moving walkways in the Denver airport. My younger son craved activities which involved motion such as car rides or escalators. I later came to realize that vibration is a soothing form of therapy for individuals with sensory disorders. For this reason, when it was time to transition away from an activity involving this type of motion, it was met with tantrum challenges. I recall one night on a family trip we were delayed in the Denver airport which has many moving walkways. Over the course of the several-hour delay, my son and I rode the moving walkways seemingly hundreds of times. When it was ultimately time to get on the plane, of course he was not ready, and it was an all-out physical battle to get him on the plane. To this day, over ten years later, I can look down at my hands to see the scratches from our struggle to get him on the plane.

I wish I could say that this was short-lived, but it went on for several years. Everyday activities like going to the store or just taking a car ride risked an aggressive outburst because he had a hard time transitioning. Our family withdrew from getting together with others for a very long time.

Our family trip to Disneyland was exemplary of this period. I would envision that most families anticipate a time of wonder and excitement for their children as they experience a Magic Kingdom seemingly just for them. From the rides to the characters, it brings a smile to most parents' faces as their children experience these moments for the first time. Unfortunately, the Anderson family trip to Disney was a moment-to-moment battle from transition to transition. Whether leaving the car or getting off the shuttle bus, each transition to the next activity was met with kicking, biting, scratching, and potentially swinging. I recall that by the time we got to our character lunch, the whole family was exhausted. I remember my wife and I were discussing whether Disney would have gluten free ice cream. It turns out that Disney is truly magical! A moment of levity in an otherwise challenging time.

After experiencing what we thought might be seizures, we visited a neurologist who delivered the diagnosis of autism spectrum disorder. This was followed by a frank opinion of what my son would probably never do: never attend typical school, never live independently, never go to college or function as a normal adult.

This is a devastating moment for any parent, and particularly for a father. It conjures many fears and dashes many hopes. I am a man of faith; however, in the face of a son suffering so much and a resolved medical opinion, I can say this was a dark time. In my view, the challenges of autism spectrum disorder or another significant developmental disorder on the father is unique. (This is not at all to diminish the impact on moms.) Fathers envision their sons playing sports and becoming independent men as adults. With every tantrum, every time my glasses were ripped from my face, every time I was kicked, was a reminder of loss. In my experience, moms are the first to engage when facing setbacks of this type, but dads can either engage or withdraw. I have seen things go both ways—some dads organize the therapies, manage the statements, and collaborate with their partner in making their child better. A child is blessed when this occurs. I have also seen dads take the opposite approach many times. Some fathers deny their child's condition, placing them in conflict with their partner who is left to address things alone. In turn, this leads to marital problems and often to divorce, leaving single parents raising special needs kids on their own.

My story developed in a hybrid fashion. Treatments for autism spectrum disorder often involve non-prescription-based treatments: diet, hyperbaric therapy, sound therapy, occupational therapy, and many others. My wife engaged in these therapies right away, doing everything and anything to make our child better. I, on the other hand, dragged my feet. For the record, I don't think I denied the diagnosis, but I didn't engage in the options necessary to make things better. Most of the therapies being proposed were things I had never heard of before, and I had lots of questions rooted in skepticism. How could something as simple as a gluten-free diet make a difference in autism? Why should we travel several hours from home in Indiana to Wisconsin to spend hours per day in a hyperbaric chamber? Why do we need to consult an out-of-town specialist when we have doctors right here in Indiana? For whatever reason, I had trouble accepting the challenge of what it would take to make things better.

Getting through this period required me to rely on the learnings I took away from my own father: whatever it takes. As difficult as things were,

I had many blessings and resources to rely upon: an accommodating employer, a great spouse, and my own parents who were supportive. Honestly, faith was the foundation that got me through this period. I remember the first time my wife sent me to the store with a gluten-free shopping list. The list was full of organic and non-processed foods which was new to me at that point in my life. The groceries cost twice as much as they had before! We tried the diet and saw modest improvement over time. By the grace of God, I latched onto this as evidence that these alternative treatments could work. Over the subsequent fifteen years, I have continued to engage and pursue anything and everything to improve my son's condition.

The Road Forward

In reflection, sharing my journey was the reason I wanted to contribute to this book. My survival as a father and husband required surrender: surrender that I was not in control, surrender that my son's path would be different than mine or the one envisioned, surrender that survival can be measured by the hour. The path to being successful as a father is a marathon and not a sprint.

While I would like to believe I would have carried these traits even without these experiences, my journey has changed my outlook on life in several profound ways. First, I have tremendous empathy for others undergoing personal challenges. Whenever I see people going through personal challenges or just acting out of character, I ask myself "what might others be going through in their life to impact their outlook in life?" Secondly, the experience has created a connection between me and the special needs community. As difficult as this has been for our family, I have had the blessings to counsel others going through these challenges. I also volunteer as a board member for two nonprofits dedicated to improving the lives of people with disabilities. My view of the world and how I engage within it has been altered in a significant way.

My younger son is now seventeen years old, and you are probably wondering how things are turning out for him. I'm pleased to report that he's an honor roll student in a neurotypical high school. He has several friends and is planning for college. He has "graduated" from all his therapies. What are the lessons learned from this father's perspective? How did I help my son, stay married, and remain employed through all of this.? I can think of three things that helped me get through these challenges:

Faith: There is no path to overcoming a challenge of this magnitude without believing in progress unseen. With each therapeutic approach, there was always a desire for the silver bullet improvement to make things better, but there never was one—progress was always one step forward and two steps back. Without faith as a source of hope, there is no way I could have helped my son get better while staying in a stable marriage.

An Open Heart: It took me some time, but as a father, I had to be open to new approaches in order for progress to be made. Everything that I had experienced before that time was conventional: parenting, education, and health. Each of those areas and many more were challenged. Had I remained inflexible in a stubborn and skeptical spirit, there is no way I could have been a constructive contributor to my son's progress.

Self-Care: Taking care of myself first may seem counterintuitive, but as the old saying goes "you can't save others if you can't save yourself." Sleep, exercise, and taking breaks (with the help of a great partner) have been key for me to approach the challenges with a positive attitude.

In conclusion, fathers can provide the foundation in the home, even in, or I should say especially in, times of challenge. A father's reaction can create a foundation for growth and confidence in the home, or it can do just the opposite. Just as my father had done for me, my responsibility was to do whatever it took for my children to go forward. Even in the face of tremendous obstacles, don't settle, even if the path is unclear.

While this was my story, I acknowledge that there are many other situations which are worse than this one. Furthermore, I have chosen to not use names in this chapter because my family, and especially my youngest son, will have their own story. I hope that one day he can share his story to inspire others.

INTRODUCING BRYANT SEATON

B ryant Seaton was born and raised in San Bernardino, California. He grew up with his mother, Janet, and sister, Wendi. In his formative years, he was an active member of the African Methodist Episcopal church as well as a talented musician and a lover of math and science.

Bryant attended the historically black college Florida A&M University (FAMU) in Tallahassee, Florida. While there, he met his amazing wife, Shondria. He was a member of the world-renowned Marching 100 at FAMU. He also became a member of Kappa Alpha Psi Fraternity Incorporated and graduated Magna Cum Laude with a degree in Computer Information Systems.

After graduating, he moved to Indianapolis to work in Information

Technology at a Pharmaceutical company. While working and raising a family, he got his master's degree in Engineering Technology from Purdue University, and became an Associate Professor at Indianapolis University Purdue University of Indianapolis. He volunteered as the High School Computer Programming team coordinator for the Indianapolis chapter of the Black Data Processing Associates. During his 23-year career, he has worked in IT in the pharmaceutical and defense industry, and recently made a career change to digital marketing.

Bryant and Shondria have two beautiful children, a son and a daughter. They've also taken on an international student from China. Bryant loves being a husband and father. He enjoys science fiction, movies, music, and technology.

NOT SORRY I'M SORRY

Introduction

Hello, my name is Bryant. I was born to my mother, a California native, and my father, a Jamaican immigrant. Their meeting and courtship was very *How Stella Got Her Groove Back*, decades before Terry McMillan decided to write about it in 1996, and Angela Bassett played Stella in the movie based on the novel. Unfortunately, like the award-winning novel and film, their relationship had struggles.

That's where I would like to start my story, at one of the most pivotal moments in my life. My parents divorced when I was ten years old. I didn't know it then, but it significantly impacted my initial attempt at fatherhood that I'll touch on later. Ultimately, I grew up like many other black children, with my mother doing most of the heavy lifting. My father didn't take the opportunity to engage with me on the level that I needed and wanted. What that looked like was missed weekends when it was his turn. I played soccer at a high level through junior high, and he rarely attended games. In junior high and high school, I became a very accomplished trombonist (concert band, ensemble band, and jazz band) and a classical soloist. I had performances all the time that were sparsely attended by my father.

I've tried to understand why he grappled with his responsibility to be a father in recent years. Unfortunately, I have come up empty and probably need to do more personal work and discuss with him to uncover the root of the issue. When talking with my mother, she indicated that he didn't have a good relationship with his father, which most likely impacted his relationship with me. Consequently, I didn't have a direct frame of reference for being a fully engaged father. What I've realized is so much of my parenting philosophy has come from what I thought a good father should be or do.

The Family

With some of my upbringing covered, let me fast forward to today. I've been married to my intelligent, wonderful, and beautiful wife, Shondria, for eighteen years. We have two exceptional children, as well as an international exchange student from China. Our son is fifteen, daughter is eleven, and the exchange student is fifteen, all at of the writing of this chapter. I believe you could consider us an average middle-class family with the same problems as everyone else. There is never enough money to go around; we're always on the run (school, dance, sports, church, fun, etc.), the existential issue of what are we going to eat for dinner tonight, fights about going to bed—you know, the standard stuff. Even in that normalcy, I experienced issues with my initial years of fatherhood. I am going to focus on the parenting of our son. Specifically, the mistakes I've made and how that has impacted me as a person and father, and my kids.

The Story

I began fatherhood extremely excited. I wanted to do the night feeding (I'm a night owl), bath time, take him to daycare and pick him up. I felt a real sense of responsibility and love for our firstborn. But I never really interrogated the sources of those emotions and actions. As he began growing out of the toddler phase, I began to have this strong desire for him to be perfect. Due to my experience and knowledge of Black people's history in America, I had a deep-down fear that the world would be tough on him as a Black boy and man. I wanted to make it as hard as possible for him to be perceived as a threat or not valuable to society. I also tried to make him the best at everything so that his intelligence and work ethic could never be questioned. As perfect a work ethic as a four-year-old could have. I constantly pushed him, berated him, and whipped him if things weren't to my ridiculous standards. I was so hard on him that even my mother, who didn't have much room to talk about being hard on children, told me that I was over the top.

It hurts to recall, but I remember a specific incident when we were on a cruise, and he was in the children's daycare for the day. When I picked him up, one of the workers told me, in broken English, that I needed to teach him how to listen better. I asked what she meant, and she said he wasn't listening to them when giving instructions. I nodded and collected my son. As soon as we got into the elevator, I began an irate tirade of yelling and whipping. So much so that he wet his pants in absolute terror. I felt like I was outside of myself watching this abuse happen. The fear on his face and anger in my voice and actions are heartbreaking to remember. I don't know how much long-term damage I did to our relationship, but I experienced the short-term damage soon after we got home.

One evening he told Shondria that he wanted her, him, and our daughter to go live somewhere else. I could stay at the house, but he wanted to leave. At a young age, he wanted nothing to do with my abusiveness. Shondria brought us all together so I could hear what my son wanted. When I heard how he felt, I was devastated. It crushed my soul to realize I was destroying my relationship with my son with my abusive behavior. Right then and there, I searched for an answer. I said a silent prayer asking God what I could do to repair this relationship. In a hushed whisper, I heard *apologize*. My initial thought was to resist, but I relented. The truth was that I was profoundly sorry for what I had done to our relationship. I just needed to accept those feelings and take the next step to begin healing.

After working through those thoughts and a brief discussion with God, I began my apology. I tried my best to let him know how sorry I was and wanted to help him understand that I really loved him. I didn't do it at the time, but I later learned to ask for forgiveness. Things didn't change immediately, but I know through the ability to apologize and ask for forgiveness, I was building trust in our relationship.

Conclusion

As I did more introspection, I realized deep down that in my attempt not to be absent, like my father, I overcorrected. That fear that I had of my kids not knowing and engaging with me turned into anger. That anger presented itself every time he wasn't meeting my high expectations. I realized that I needed to adopt new behavior with my children going forward. In each interaction, I endeavor to realize when I'm losing it and immediately apologize for bad behavior, angry outbursts, etc. I'm constantly seeking to strike the difficult balance of holding them accountable for their mistakes (or their bad behavior) and apologizing if my initial reaction was out of line.

When I've said sorry and asked for forgiveness for losing my temper, I have demonstrated to them how to deal with anger and focus on better behavior. I have come to realize that there is no more significant growth than recognizing your faults and mistakes and admitting them to your children. When you follow that up with an apology and a request for forgiveness, it is amazing the level of intimacy and engagement you can have with your children. The best part about all this is if you teach them by example, this learned behavior can improve their relationships in the future. They can be more self-reflective, which can create healthy interactions with others. Now, if I look back at my original fear of not being engaged, I started in the wrong direction, creating more disengagement. Through learning to apologize, I've conquered that fear. Ultimately, I'm not sorry that I'm sorry!

INTRODUCING LAMAR EASON

Lamar Eason was born in Willingboro, New Jersey on August 18, 1980, to Louis and Lanette Eason. He grew up in a military family, moving often. Though he didn't always appreciate the moves, he did grow to appreciate the diversity in the world as well as the many great things to see. Throughout his childhood, he grew up in multiple states in the US and countries across the world. Upon graduation from high school, Lamar attended Illinois College where he earned a Bachelor of Arts. With this degree, he became a teacher where he has been an educator at all grade levels from primary to twelfth.

After several years of teaching, Lamar taught abroad in Kenya, Africa. Upon his return to the states, he continued his education and earned a Master's in Educational Leadership. It was during this time that he met his forever partner and better half, Jenna, a Canadian. They were married on June 6, 2009, in Wolfville, Nova Scotia. Upon finishing his first Master's Degree, Lamar, Jenna, and their two children at the time moved from Springfield, Illinois to Caledonia, Nova Scotia, where Lamar took a Vice-Principal position at North Queens Community School. Since that time, he has been the RCH (Race, Culture and Human Rights) Coordinator for the South Shore School Board in Bridgewater, Nova Scotia, and is now the Principal at Bayview Community School in Mahone Bay, Nova Scotia.

Lamar has been married to Jenna Eason for thirteen years and currently lives in Bridgewater. He has five amazing children. Like many, he could not and would not be the father that he is without the support and love from his amazing wife. Together, all things are possible!

FIVE GOLDEN AXIOMS OF FATHERHOOD

We had been married about a year when Jenna, my wife, first told me that we were gonna have a baby. It's funny the things that run through your head. Jenna and I had been camping and she broke the news to me on our trip. I think I stood there, paused, mouth open, for what felt like an eternity. I don't know what it's like for all fathers, but I can tell you for me a lot ran through my mind. I thought of what kind of father I wanted to be. I thought of what kind of father I didn't want to be. And most importantly, I thought, "Holy crap! I'm going to be responsible for a person!"

As the initial news settled in, I began to think of all the things that I would need to be a good father. Even now, with five children, I still think daily about the type of person I am and the type of person I want my children to know me as. I recognize that every decision I make and every action I may carry out impacts them. These are the things that keep you up at night as a father, as a parent.

There's a documentary called *Dads* and there is a scene where Will Smith talks about the first time he learned he was going to be a father. He talks about it so eloquently: as he says, "we get a thousand-page manual for a TV, and they send us home with a baby... and nothing!"

For fathers, both that are to be or who already are, this is a brotherhood. None of us has all the answers. None of us knows the exact way, but together we are stronger. We may not have a thousand-page manual; however, we have the learned experiences of the past, present, and future. Each child you are blessed with yields a new lesson with every passing moment. Enjoy the moments. My contribution to that 'manual' is these five lessons I've learned as a father of five. Now, I am not claiming to know it all, but am hoping that by sharing a little, it can add to the brotherhood's experience.

Layla (Beautiful night)

When we had our children, we named them with intention. Layla was born at 11:23pm at night. It was surreal to finally have a child. It was, after all the nurses had left and doctors were gone, a beautiful night. After months of waiting, we finally had our baby, but the process we went through before having her is funny to look back on.

It is true that when you have multiple children, you treat the first very differently than the last. With Layla, we went to parenting classes (which I do recommend, especially with your first). We bought things that I laugh about now. Things that parents do not need, but as new parents, you certainly think you do! We had a wipe warmer, a diaper genie, swings, and slings galore. We had things that we bought. We had things that other people bought. We had things that we never even touched because it was all just too much. What I realize now is that we had everything we needed. Love. As cliche as it sounds, we were so excited for Layla to come that we were overprepared. Now, I'm not suggesting it's a bad thing to be prepared, but what we needed most was to make sure that we were mentally prepared. This is no easy feat.

My wife and I learned that patterns in raising children can help each child and they have laid the groundwork for some successes. As an example, with food, our pediatrician said that babies will eat when they are hungry. Now, this sounds like a very obvious thing, but as a new parent, it was hard at times to make meals that Layla would eat. We weren't sure if we should be making separate or different meals for her, so we ended up feeding her the same foods that we ate. We ate pretty healthy, balanced meals and didn't make anything extra for our baby girl. To this day, Layla, like all of our kids, will try anything. Food is not an issue. It is the pattern that we have set.

These patterns are what kept us sane. When it came to sleep, we set a pattern early. In our partnership, I got the kids at night when they would wake and give them to Jenna when she was breastfeeding. It was a partnership. We set patterns and relied on each other. We tried to be as consistent as possible, even though I worked and Jenna stayed home with the baby. I knew that I had to step up for both of them.

I remember one day when I came home from work, I had had a long day. My wife came to give me a hug right when I walked in the door. I just wanted some space and time to decompress from my day (spent around children no less), which is the case for many fathers with the same work/home arrangement that we have. What I realize now is that she needed companionship. She was with the baby all day and needed her partner. To this day I regret getting frustrated and saying that I don't want hugs when I walk in the door. The truth is, I had made it about me and missed that I couldn't only be focused on my needs now. I had a wife and a baby whose needs came before my own. I still know that I need time and space, and I find healthy ways of getting it. But reflecting on this interaction, I learned that fatherhood and being a good partner are about commitment and putting my family above myself.

Fatherhood has changed my friends. As dads, we can't go to work, come home, decompress, and go to bed. We have to be men that set examples for our children and other dads. I want to be a father that is at games, pick-ups, knows my kids' friends, helps with making lunches for school, and more. Every day, fatherhood is a commitment and from that first moment at 11:23pm on January 27 when Layla entered my life, I knew I had to be better. So my first lesson to my fathers out there is to commit to this life. Put it all out there day after day for fatherhood. Set the example and be there. Everyday.

Lesson #1: Commit to fatherhood every day

Sawyer (Woodcutter)

When we began going to parenting classes for our first child, I remember the instructor saying, "children will give you a degree in patience." This could be no further from the truth with Sawyer. Sawyer knows how to put me through the wringer! Diagnosed with anxiety and ADHD, my amazing son is both smart and short-sighted. At the age of two, he would put puzzles together faster than his big sister Layla could. He sees patterns in learning and reads people like a detective. With all of his strengths, the anxiety and ADHD can cause him to miss the feelings and emotions of others. Sometimes he can see it. Sometimes he can't. One of the downsides of this is that he has a hard time seeing the perspective of others.

When you have a child that has challenges, it is natural to think about what you have done as a parent for this to happen. I remember when my wife and I learned of Sawyer's diagnosis, we had long discussions about what we thought we did. I can remember thinking on many occasions, "what did I do to make him this way?" When he had a tantrum at night, when he said he hated himself or that we didn't love him, we would get through it, and then I would reflect, what could I have done differently? What I have learned over the years is that the answer is simple. There are some things that, as a father, you have no control over. As a control freak, I have a hard time with this—can any of you fellas relate? I want to fix things. I want to make them better and I believe any good father thinks about this every day. But fixing it is not what Sawyer needs. Many kids don't need anything fixed. What they need is someone to be there, to listen, to give a hug, and to support. Being a father means that you are there and willing to put in the work, and sometimes not get to a solution, at least not in the way you think the solution should look.

One night I can remember, Sawyer was having a particularly hard time accepting a consequence. This is often the case because he struggles with understanding another's perspective, and he often only sees things through his lens. In this particular case, he could not see that his actions had an impact on one of his siblings and the consequence was that he lost out on our family movie night. Because he felt wronged, he attempted to make sure that no one got to see/watch the movie. For the next hour and a half, I sat with Sawyer as he yelled hurtful things, hit the wall, and attempted to watch the movie. Through this whole process, I tried to stay calm. I spoke a few words and I just watched him. I remember this being the first time that the lightbulb went off. Up to this point, as a fixer, I was trying to reason with someone that couldn't be reasoned with when frustrated. I was trying to "talk sense" into him. What I needed to do was be patient. I needed to not fix the problem, but be present for the problem. I needed to listen when he calmed down and ride the wave. I needed to *not* exercise my authority as his father, and in doing so, I learned that there is usually some underlying reason he explodes or reacts the way he does. In this case, it was guilt. I have uncovered that it is often guilt or embarrassment, a sense of low self-worth, or a lack of feeling loved. With Sawyer, as with most of my kids, if I am just there for them, versus trying to fix something, I get further. Am I always patient? Hell no! Am I working on it every day? Hell yes. And to be a good dad, you have to.

Lesson #2: Be patient.

Everett (Wild like a boar)

I could talk for days about the lessons that I have learned from Everett. Our experiences with him have shaped our family in ways I don't think I will ever be able to fully explain.

At eight months pregnant, my wife was feeling very uncomfortable. Being the third child, she had been through all of this before, but this time felt different. In fact, people would tell her that she looked like she was ready to have the baby any day, and she would respond, "I actually have two months left until the due date." My poor wife was miserable. I tried to help and comfort her with the multiple body pillows in bed and massages. I did what I could, but nothing helped.

At the time, we were seeing a midwife. Our first two children were born by C-section and she was adamant about not having another one. As a husband, it is hard (understatement of the century) to watch your wife have an unplanned C-section. There are many physical complications such as picking up the baby, driving, and infections from the surgery and neither she nor I wanted to go through that again. While Jenna didn't want another C-section, many OB-GYN's will not allow for a vaginal birth after having had a c-section, so now you know why we were seeing a midwife. Everything was moving smoothly until one ultrasound, where they found something wasn't quite right.

They ended up sending us to the IWK, a children's hospital in Halifax. There we had an ultrasound where they discovered that Everett's esophagus was not connected to his stomach. He had a condition called a tracheoesophageal fistula. The impact of this condition on Jenna was that there was no cycling of the amniotic fluid in the womb, and so the fluid building up was the reason for the discomfort. The doctor told us that we would not be leaving the hospital that night and they would have to drain the fluid. They also shared that when Everett was born, he would need surgery immediately. As I heard this news, I felt overwhelmed. We had two other kids that we had to think about. What do we do with them? What happens when he is born? We lived an hour and a half from the hospital. How were we going to do this? As the doctor left the room for us to talk, we both sat in shock. We knew this was going to be hard, but we were in this together. After some time, we composed ourselves and moved forward. That night, they drained multiple litres of fluid from Jenna's stomach. Over the next couple of weeks, we went back to the hospital three times. They drained a total of eighteen litres over four visits. At thirty-six weeks, we went in for a planned C-section.

On October 21, Everett was born, and looking back at the pictures always gives me chills. Everett had his surgery and for the next month, lived at the children's hospital in the neonatal intensive care unit (NICU), the pediatric intensive care unit (PICU), and then finally a regular room. We figured out childcare. Sometimes I would drive to the city after work, stay for the night with him next to his incubator while Jenna slept, and in the morning drive back to work. We had an amazing family that supported us and friends that we could rely on (this is key—find your village and lean on them when you need to). We were lucky to be able to stay at the Ronald McDonald housing located near the hospital since we didn't live in the city. Through all of this, we found strength in each other and our faith. Today, we have a little boy who is maybe one of the most resilient people that I know. I believe that this is because of what he has been through already in his short life. I think that is also true for me. With each trial and challenge of fatherhood, we grow. Putting my faith and believing in something other than me is important in growing as a father.

Lesson #3: Always believe and have faith in something bigger

Oliver (Olive Branch - Peace)

After three C-sections, we finally found a doctor who was willing to let Jenna try for a natural birth. This was almost unheard of. He was an amazing doctor and we felt comfortable from the start. For the first time, the process just seemed right. Even though Ollie was two weeks late, when we went to the hospital with contractions, everything just felt right. From parking the car to holding Oliver, it was less than an hour and when I held him for the first time, there was an overwhelming sense of calm. His name fits him perfectly!

If you ask any of my family members who are most like me, Oliver would most likely be the answer. Of all my children, Oliver was the one that would go to me instead of Jenna. We have always had this connection. When he was one, we flew to a family graduation. Oliver wouldn't go to anyone but me. While people tried and tried to pry him away from me, he wouldn't let me out of his sight. Even to this day, he would snuggle with me every night if he could.

When they say that children can be the payback from your childhood, they were talking about Oliver! As the youngest of seven, I think back to the torture I caused my siblings and parents. I wasn't a bad kid, but boy was I the baby of the family! For a while, Oliver was just that... the youngest, and he ate it up. He has always been a charmer. He has a contagious laugh and a smile that keeps people smiling.

One of my childhood memories is that my father was never okay with backtalk. Even when it was joking, he struggled to see it as anything but disrespect. I try to be a more fun dad and allow my kids to express themselves, but find myself sometimes following this same behaviour as my father. One time, I was trying to be serious and talk to the kids, and Oliver looked at me with a straight face and said, "Shush it down, dad," and then began laughing. As serious as I was, I couldn't help but laugh. This is Ollie's superpower. He can disarm even the most frustrated person and in those moments, I have to remember that he is a child that just wants laughter and smiles to be a part of everyone's day. Being his father, I try to support this even on my hardest day and the best thing I can do is let his light shine.

Lesson #4: Let them be your light and focus on the good

Emery (Brave):

And then there were five!

Emery was born on Labor day and as a workaholic, I think there was some irony in this. After Emery, I knew that I was done with having children. I knew that five was the perfect number. We talked about more, but I felt that what I could give each child as a father was set at the number five.

And then COVID-19 hit. The best part about the global pandemic for me was when everything shut down, I could spend days with my family. It slowed down our lives. For maybe the first time in my fatherhood life, I was able to be present, like *really* present. I think that it was also the first time that I was able to spend large amounts of time with my family without having a sense of guilt about all the other responsibilities I had. The world shut down and it was great! Even now, I don't think that I maximized that time together. I would still like to have done more than we did, but I was able to make journals with the kids, do crafts, go on nature walks, play in the yard, and just talk. I believe the global pandemic helped to give Emery his personality. It created an atmosphere that drove us together as a family. Emery had us all at his beck and call. While he is only three at this point, I have been there for more of the moments of his life than my other kids and, at times, it makes me sad that it took something like a pandemic to bring me to this realization about how important these moments are. Because of this, I try hard not to take this time with my greatest gifts for granted. Knowing that Emery is our last child, I try to live every moment with all of them to the best of my ability. I am more aware now that each moment is maybe the last. The last first step. The last first tooth. The last. We won't get these times again, so I live now for each of them.

Lesson #5: Live for the moment. You don't get them back.

I believe that the lessons that I have learned from all of my children over time have made me a better person and a better father. I am calmer in my interactions with them and I can see things through a different lens after almost eleven years of fatherhood. As these qualities set in as a parent, I have become someone who can be a more present and aware father. I don't get it right all the time, maybe even most of the time. I make mistakes. I yell and raise my voice. I have regrets. The biggest regret that I have, though, is not taking more time to be with them. Work is important, but not as important as them. I don't want to be the father that looks back and doesn't have memories of my kids' youth. I don't want my children to only call mom when they are in a jam. I want my children to remember me as the dad that was present. Every day I grow. Every day as a father, I learn. I hope that every day

I am a little bit better than the day before. I will never be a perfect father, but I will always be a father working to be perfect for them.

INTRODUCING JAMES M. LEWIS

James Lewis is a husband, married to Marla Lewis for twenty-seven years, and father of two children, a son and daughter. James was raised in southern Indiana and grew up being parented by Jim and Joyce Lewis, and brother to Jennifer. As a child, James was known to be both a troublemaker and problem solver and always enjoyed learning. He was grounded well in the church, attending St James United Methodist most of his life and participating in the spiritual, administrative, and social aspects of his home church.

Being inquisitive by nature, James excelled in science and attended the University of Louisville and graduated with both bachelor's and master's degrees in chemical engineering. Shortly after graduating, James met Marla, and married a few years after moving to Pensacola, Florida together to begin their married life and career journey.

Over the past twenty years, James has been blessed to have Marla by his side and the two have raised two great children, received their MBAs from Purdue, and worked for various industries. They have also enjoyed living in several cities, learning new locales, and making new friends.

PRESENCE

Before I give my two cents on fatherhood, a little about myself: Looking back, I had few complaints about my younger years. I grew up in a two-parent home, with both parents working and a younger sister to pick on when I got bored. I didn't think about my circumstances at the time, but was fortunate enough to be around two great-grandmas, grandparents on both sides, aunts, uncles, first and second cousins, and play cousins (those that you didn't know weren't really cousins till you grew up). My dad worked shift work most of my life and I could pretty easily tell you when he was working day, swing, or night shift. The only time he was not around was swing shift: 3:00 pm – 11:00 pm. My sister and I would come home from school and he would already be at work. I remember my dad not being the outdoorsman, being good at everything else, and being able to impress anyone he met, including my friends. Whenever he'd come to a grade school function, my friends would always ask, "does your Dad play football?" In a weak moment, I'd live in the gray area and say "not anymore." He was always handy and when push came to shove (i.e. he could do it without paying a contractor), was good at general handyman work. My mother was a licensed physical therapist and most of the time worked for facilities that helped people with disabilities, many of whom were kids. She did stereotypical suburban mom stuff—was den mother for my cub scouts, participated in United Methodist Women, and kept my sister and I fed, clothed, and educated. One of the things I appreciated most was her taking us to the library. She would always have checked out what seemed like a dozen romance novels and would go find more, while I would not want to be with her and go find books on my own.

I read everything from books on battleships to *Lord of the Rings*, to how to program in Basic.

I finished 6th out of 290 in my class; if I recall correctly, better than most and not as high as my ego would have liked. I always succeeded but still wonder, did I push myself or apply myself like I could have? There is always doubt; what ifs? What if I pushed myself harder? What if I had a different guidance counselor? What if I stuck with sports? What if I didn't mind being out front?

I finished high school as one of two African Americans in my class. Went on to college and graduated with a master's degree as the only African American in my chemical engineering program and followed up with an M.B.A. and was the only African American in my graduating class. As I have frequently been the one of few among many, I have tried to impart the ability to both stand up on their own as the individual African American in the room and the individual who others look up to.

I think of two things considering my history when I reflect on my style and approach to fatherhood—presence and the ability to be way more than average every day.

Presence

If I could advise any father, I would start by telling them to make every effort to be there for their child. A dad being in a child's life, especially a black child, is likely the absolute best thing a father can do. For me, this started when my children were born—you name the activity, I'm there. My son played soccer and since I was at every practice, I helped coach. He wanted to be in cub scouts and needed a parent to lead—I was there. My daughter wanted to play lacrosse, so we bought lacrosse gear for both of us and learned together. When she did competitive dance, I attended each local and away competition. Maintaining presence is more profound than being fiscally responsible for a child. Money is necessary, but the time is required and remembered. The benefit of being an active parent in your child's life will outweigh anything you can buy. Speaking from the perspective of someone who grew up with a father and mother who did not hover but were involved in every event and present for all activities, I firmly believe we all would choose to have a father involved in every activity and available for support over anything else.

Growing up, my dad never was far. He didn't travel for his job and very rarely we were not face-to-face daily. How else was I to get to football, baseball, orchestra, or the barbershop? While I'm not sure if it was a conscious decision or not, once I had children I didn't travel as a part of my job until they were grade- and middle-school age. While my trips were normally a few days here and there, many of my trips involved helping with math homework over the phone or in an extreme case, flying my son to meet me for his college visit. Dad also was around for others and this did not go unnoticed by me. He was a lay leader at church, church treasurer, and problem solver for many in the family. Both my sister and I saw him respond to others as well as take care of others without asking for anything in return.

Thinking about my dad today, I ask myself frequently about the pushing of stories of Black people growing up without contact with their fathers. You get stories about star athletes growing up fatherless, but few stories, with notable exceptions—Richard Williams and Tiger Woods come to mind—include fathers, and even in these cases, the story quickly goes to how the father is not there.

I hope, as black fathers, we can control our narrative on our role. My few words here are only a start. Sharing my few thoughts on fatherhood is helpful to me as well as a part of the story we can craft together. For me, maintaining a presence in my kids' lives is the most important message I can share.

More than Average

If I do my job right as a dad, my kids will be a better version of their mother and me. I've never asked my father why we share the same first name but I am not a junior. As I understand, he is not a fan of the name "Junior," but I also think part of it is that even though we carry the same formal first name, we are known as two different names and that helps me be my own person as much as possible, and being Junior could hinder that.

My son and daughter deserve to walk their own path and my job is to help them. That being said, I have higher expectations for them than for myself. While not overtly pushing, I have always asked both children to not settle. Not to do the bare minimum. While we may get average in some areas as a result, the intent is to strive for more. As a black kid in an environment where you have eyes on you every day, striving for average is perceived as not working hard enough. Part of my purpose as a dad is to push when you see gaps and present challenges when you see opportunity.

It's likely that I settled for average in my life, or at least the appearance of average at times. Having children who are extremely observant compounds this lesson. How do you push a child to be better when you have not done so yourself? The honest answer is, you find a way. It may be love, it may be simple guidance or even space. But as a dad, your job is to navigate through the options and help your child understand not only the benefit of being the best they can be, but also the need to be the best they can.

Being The Example

The lessons I learned both overtly and by observation from my father have influenced every action and breath I've taken as a father. I've been blessed with an amazing wife and the opportunity to be a father to two awesome children., all the while challenging me to be a better man, father, and husband, and re-assessing my choices as I go through life. As a dad, helping your child to develop their own greatness and being there and present as a father is the way God has helped me be a parent.

Summary

Some of what I have learned about being a father can be related to being the engineer that is my profession. In my role we have control loops like a thermostat: in the room, as you observe something is not normal or where you want it to be, you make a change in setpoint and the system tries to adjust to your new setpoint. Being a father has in many ways operated the same, as I continuously have monitored my children's environment and their performance and when course correction needed, attempted to make a change in setpoint. This was either through my presence, asking them to be more, or being the example. What I needed to do was make sure the input I gave to my children were in line with my expectations. Change may not occur at the pace that I envisioned, but as my wife and I had put in the presence, pushes to do more, and examples of humanity we desired, we both had faith in the positive outcome.

Stacia Gowens et al.

INTRODUCING RYAN MCMILLAN

Ryan McMillan is the proud father of Carter McMillan and husband to Meg McMillan. He is also a financial professional with ten years of experience in the industry. He is currently becoming a financial advisor.

Born in Lansing, Michigan, Ryan decided not to follow his family's Spartan legacy at Michigan State University and moved west to California. He attended California State University, Long Beach where he received his B.S in Business Marketing.

After college, Ryan moved to San Diego where he met his wife, Meg. While they were still dating, Ryan and Meg left California and went on an adventure to Asia, living in Taiwan for fifteen months. They both were English teachers for children during their travels and visited sixteen countries together.

Ryan is a new father and loves being a dad. "What makes you a man is not the ability to make a child, it's the courage to raise one," said Barack Obama. Ryan grew up in a close family, so becoming a father is something he had always aspired to be one day.

Ryan's strength is having the ability to listen and connect with people from all walks of life. He is grateful for the support from his family and friends as he continues to build his legacy.

THE UNCERTAINTY OF FATHERHOOD

There is no official blueprint for becoming a father. It's challenging, unpredictable, frustrating, and exhausting. At the same time, it's incredible, unconditional, fun, silly, phenomenal, and one of the best experiences in life.

It All Starts With Me

Growing up in Lansing, Michigan, my brother and I were fortunate to have both our mother and father. My parents were married for forty-three beautiful years and gave us the foundation for how to love your family. I'm so grateful my father decided to be present and raise his two black kings. From teaching me how to ride a bike to volunteering as a coach for my elementary basketball team, my father was there. I knew one day when I started my own family, I would want to be completely involved in their lives.

I'm Gonna Be A Dad!

In December 2020, my wife and I welcomed our amazing son Carter. Earlier that year, we all experienced a global pandemic as COVID-19 rapidly spread across the world. A few weeks after the lockdown happened, we found out that my wife was pregnant. We both stood in our bathroom anxiously waiting for the results of the pregnancy test. Our initial reaction was shock as we both stared at the two lines on the test. Looking back at it now, we laugh about how we thought my wife's moodiness and exhaustion was from being quarantined. My wife and I wanted children, but we talked about waiting another year. God had different plans for us.

Several thoughts raced through my mind as I was about to take this new journey of fatherhood. One of the first thoughts I had was of my mother, who unexpectedly passed in 2017. Knowing my mother would not physically be here with her first grandchild and seeing her son take on this new role as a father made me feel sad and I cried. Although I was happy, nervous, and excited about becoming a father, not having my mother around to share this experience was hard for me.

My mother, Deborah McMillan, was only 5' 2", but she moved mountains. She was a phenomenal woman who loved her family so much. She was not only my mom, but a kindergarten teacher to many children and made a big difference in her community and the world. My mom really cared so much about the next generation and spent her whole life dedicated to improving the lives of her students and families. Nurturing my son has come natural to me and I owe that to my mom. She was a natural nurturer to many children, and I got to witness this over the years. I remember a time when I was a child, my mom asked me if she could take my old winter coats to her school. She explained to me that some of her students came to school without a coat and could really use one. If you have ever experienced a Michigan winter, then you know that time of the year can be extremely cold. I was happy to give my coats to my mom's students and was happy knowing this was the kind of person she was, so giving and altruistic. I miss my mom deeply, and at times when I look at my son, I can see her. Carter is still connected with his grandma in heaven. We have a photo of her on our wall that he waves to every morning, and we will continue to tell stories about her life as he grows up.

Uncertainty comes with being a new father and pretty much *every* other aspect of life. Sometimes, events don't happen according to plan. For example—our gender reveal. We had to host it on Zoom due to the pandemic. Our family and friends joined us on video for this exciting moment. One person that couldn't make it, unfortunately, was my wife's father, Ron. My father-in-law became ill that very same day and had to be hospitalized. His illness wasn't COVID-19 related, but he did need heart surgery and was in and out of the hospital for a few months. During this time, I did my best to keep the level of stress down for my wife and our growing baby boy. I did not have control of this situation and at times I felt helpless. I tried to think of how I could make this better for my wife, but all I could do was comfort her and be present. On October 1, 2020, we lost my wife's father, two months before our bouncing baby boy was born.

As a new father, I believed certain people in my life would still be here. For me, two of these people were my mother and my father-in-law. Our son now has two guardian angels looking over and protecting him. In my short experience of fatherhood, I'm learning that times of uncertainty will continue to happen. It's how you respond when they occur because usually, you will not be in control.

And The Uncertainty Continues To Mount

The pandemic still being in full effect, there were many other unexpected and unprecedented first-time dad-to-be challenges. During my wife's hospital appointments, I wasn't allowed to come into the hospital to check on the progress of my wife's pregnancy. I would patiently wait outside, while my wife would call me to allow me to ask any questions I may have. Heck, I was new to this too and many of you can relate to having all the questions when you were expecting your first child!

Thankfully, I was able to be in the room when our son was born. *"From the hospital that first night, took an hour just to get the car seat in right."* Will Smith from his infamous song "Just the Two of Us." I definitely could relate to these lyrics as a new dad. This was the first time I had to properly install a car seat and the struggle was real. I needed our nurse to help me out before we could even leave the hospital. I can confidently say today that I'm a pro at installing my son's car seat. Due to the pandemic, our doctor advised us for the first six weeks of Carter's life that we should avoid being around anyone, including family. This was difficult because our family and friends were so excited to meet our baby boy, but we did what was best and limited being around people for a few months. At the end of the day, I'm happy my wife and son are healthy.

Handling The Unexpected Like A Boss Dad

With my son, I have made the choice to be involved in his life every day. Waking up at three in the morning when I'm completely exhausted and my son is crying because he needs a diaper change. Bathing him before bed and reading a story together. Making silly faces at each other at the table when it's time to eat. Taking him on a stroll through our neighborhood so he can explore. Having dance parties in our living room and saying, "Hey Alexa, play Carter's playlist." I do all of this because I want to continue to build the bond between my son and me. I also want my son to remember that his father has been there for him since day one, just as my father was.

To all the new dads, remember this: becoming a father is a new experience you continue to learn from as your kids grow and change. As soon as you feel you got the hang of fatherhood, suddenly it changes again. There have been moments in my own fatherhood journey when I was not always sure if I was doing things right. Questions I have asked myself: Will I be a good father? Am I doing enough? Will I teach my son the right things? I have had to remind myself it's okay to not have it all figured out in the beginning because you will grow as a father if you choose to stay involved.

INTRODUCING ERIC HODGE

Eric Hodge has been a Certified HUD REAC Inspector since 2009. Prior to consulting for HUD, Eric held various accounting positions for major property management and development firms. He was personally responsible for the fiscal duties for portfolios of Real Property totaling over 13,000 units with assets valued at over $1.3 billion.

In addition, Eric previously owned and managed a number of single-family units in the Philadelphia Metropolitan area. Eric holds dual bachelor's degrees in Accounting & Management from Temple

University.

Eric Has been married to his beautiful wife Nichole for 24 years, and they have two children, Eric Nicholas and Taylor Alexis.

DADDY

"Does it ever feel kinda weird to you when he calls you that?"

"Calls me what?"

"When he calls you 'Mommy.' Have you gotten used to it? It's not a little weird to you?"

"I don't know, maybe a little. Why? You think it's *weird*? Like in a bad way?"

"Oh no! Not 'weird' in a bad way at all. It's just crazy that this little person is calling *me* 'Daddy.' It still gets to me. It's cool."

"And two years later you're just figuring out how cool it is?"

That was circa 1996, and that little person who was the subject of all of my wife's and my attention and conversation that day was Lil' Eric, my Baby Boy. My two-year-old little guy, running around with my exact face, a carbon copy, my very own mini-me. I'm sure that that moment was like many others that I'd had over the two years since his birth; moments that I looked at him and thought, "I'm actually someone's Dad."

Becoming "Dad"

Eric Nicholas Hodge came into this world on December 8, 1993, at 9:49 AM weighing a whopping 3 pounds, 11 ounces. Nicky (my then girlfriend, now wife) had been hospitalized for nearly three months before his birth. I remember juggling my new position as a staff accountant, visiting Nick (the name I call my wife, Nichole) at Pennsylvania Hospital every day after work, and studying for the CPA exam in her hospital room—all while awaiting the birth of our first child. Eric arrived two months premature and had to spend twenty-four days in the neonatal intensive care unit (NICU). I was in the operating room during the planned C-section and watched the very moment he entered the world. They showed Nick his face quickly, then a team of doctors, nurses, and respiratory therapists quickly transported him to the NICU, and I was right on their heels. I stayed with him all day. We still laugh about the fact that after Baby Boy got here, Nicky was on her own in that hospital! I spent the entire day just watching him and talking to him as he lay in an incubator. The nursing staff sent polaroid pictures of me with Eric up to her room as she recovered from the surgery that day. For the rest of her stay, and after she was discharged, Nick would spend all day at the hospital with Eric, and I would relieve her when I got off work, spending the rest of the evening with him. Every evening from 6:00 pm to midnight, I sat holding him and sometimes feeding him with a tiny tube that went down his nostril into his belly. We finally brought him home on New Year's Eve weighing only 4 pounds. That thwarted my plans, and I never would become a CPA.

I was going on twenty-six years old when Eric was born, and looking back, we had the benefit of inexperience to shield us from some of the effects of the challenges that we endured with a high-risk pregnancy and a tiny newborn. I don't remember being especially worried about Eric or Nick, to be honest. I think we both thought that her high-risk status just meant that she needed more care to bring our baby into the world safely. We never questioned whether he would actually survive. To be honest, we simply had no point of reference for that kind of stress at that point. That was a gift and unfortunately, that would change.

We got married when Eric was four years old, and a year later we had a miscarriage. A year after that, to our surprise, we were pregnant again. This time Nick spent the entire pregnancy on bed rest, and the last four months hospitalized. She was admitted to the hospital in December and came out in April. Our daughter Taylor Alexis was born on March 29, 2001, at 4:35 pm weighing 4 pounds, 3 ounces, and just like her big brother, I followed the medical staff from the operating room to the nursery, leaving my wife once again. But although Taylor was completely healthy and able to leave the hospital with us a few days later, this was the pregnancy that showed us how fragile our pregnancies actually were, and there were many scares during those four months in the hospital. Nevertheless, I was now the father of a seven-year-old and a beautiful newborn baby girl, both miracles.

It's hard to really capture how difficult the next decade would prove to be and to be honest, I'm not sure how we survived it. In the spring of 2003, Eric, age nine, was pulled backward while attempting to jump off a jungle gym during recess. He suffered a near-fatal brain injury that would leave him on life support. Just like we had at the beginning of his life, Nick and I stayed with him around the clock in the intensive care unit, only leaving to shower and care for his two-year-old baby sister. I'll spare you all the details, but Eric again made a miraculous recovery, though he was left with debilitating migraine headaches and some major organizational issues that would follow him for quite some time.

Navigating and Leading through Loss

In 2007, we were thrilled to find out we were expecting again, but just as we entered the third trimester, during a prenatal visit, the baby's heartbeat was gone. In 2009 we were again expecting. On April 8, 2010, after two months in the hospital, our baby girl Brooke was born. She died the very next day. My life was turned upside down. I was devastated and completely broken, but I spent the next few days planning a funeral, taking care of my children who were grieving, and trying my best to take care of my wife who was still hospitalized and completely inconsolable.

Nick needed me to pray for her because she couldn't bring herself to do it, but the truth is I was grieving and found it hard to talk to God during this time. We had faith and we really believed that Brooke was going to live, and we were confused and let down when she passed. I spent the next few weeks, and years quite honestly, trying my best to help my wife and my children recover from the loss of Brooke. Sometimes I did really well, like when I successfully intercepted the mail so that Nick wouldn't see Brooke's birth certificate or her death certificate. I have them hidden and she still has never laid eyes on them. I would go out of my way to avoid driving by the cemetery where she is buried. Nick still can't drive in that direction. It was years before Nicky was strong enough to hear that I had been visiting our little girl's gravesite regularly, and continue to do so.

Then there were times when, quite frankly, I blew it. A few days after Brooke's funeral, I decided that my wife needed to leave the house. She was in a lot of emotional and physical pain while still recovering from the surgery. I convinced her to go to the mall because she needed to walk around. She was resistant, primarily because she didn't feel that she looked like herself.

"Don't worry about how you look! The only person who you need to impress is me, and I'm right here with you." And with that, she agreed to go.

Fumble #1

We arrived at the mall, and Nick made a few more comments about her appearance and how she was concerned that someone would see her. Again, I assured her that she looked fine. We were walking hand in hand, window shopping, talking about things other than our loss, and for the first time in over a week, my wife finally started smiling.

I'm just going to go on ahead and claim temporary insanity for the events that happened next. As we were walking through the mall and my wife is talking to me, I interrupted her mid-sentence,

"Hey, Leah! That's Leah from around the way."

I had spotted a woman who grew up in my neighborhood walking several yards in front of us, and without even thinking, I called her. Leah stopped, turned around, and saw me. At that very moment, Nick slowly turns to look at me, eyes welling up. Leah walks back toward us and greets me with a huge hug.

"Hey, Rick!" Leah says with a smile.

"Leah, this is my wife, Nicky. Nicky, this is Leah." If my wife responded, I certainly didn't hear it.

"Hey, Beautiful," Leah says while giving Nick a clearly unwelcomed hug.

After a few more seconds of pleasantries, Leah left. She was the lucky one.

"Who the hell was that? And why would you do that?" Nick was crying now. "I'm ready to go, NOW! Why would you do this to me? I told you I didn't want to see anyone!"

She was right. She did tell me that.

"Babe, what did I do?!" I asked.

"What do you mean, what did you do? Are you crazy!" "Yeah, a little", I thought to myself.

"Why was it necessary to call out to your *girlfriend* while you're walking with your WIFE? And why is that trick calling me *beautiful*?"

Oh! My! God! I had really stepped in it.

"Girlfriend? She was never my girlfriend. Babe, I haven't seen that girl in twenty years."

"And you couldn't wait another damn day? She was walking in front of us, and you could have easily ignored her, but NO! You had to call the bitch back to us, didn't you? DIDN'T YOU?"

"Now Babe, why you callin' the girl a bitch? Listen, let's…"

"Oh, so *now* you're defending her? Tell me this, how the hell did you recognize her from the back *anyway*?"

At this point, Nick was crying hard in the middle of the mall, and I knew I had to get her home.

"C'mon Babe," as I took her by the hand. "Let's go home. I'm so sorry."

The very situation she wanted to avoid, I had unintentionally created. She was grief-stricken and exhausted and didn't want anyone to see her in that condition. Nicky told me later that she was humiliated about her appearance, and hurt that I would engage someone in a conversation when I knew how she was feeling. She said everyone else has a new baby to explain their postpartum appearance—and she didn't. That was a rough day. But as time went by, the days got brighter and while we even laugh about the Leah incident now, it took years for our family to heal from Brooke's death. Brooke's birthday is still somewhat difficult for all of us, especially my wife.

Fumble #2

A few years ago, I noticed that Nick was getting a little sad as we approached April 8th, Brooke's birthday, so I called her on my way home from work,

"Hey Babe, get ready. I'm taking you somewhere tonight."

"Where?" she asked. She sounded excited.

"Don't worry about it. Just get ready."

"Ok!"

I picked her up and she jumped in the car grinning, and she was all dressed up. I started getting a little nervous.

"Babe, you really are dressed up, aren't you?"

"Yes! You sure you don't want to tell me where we're going? Never mind, don't tell me. I want to be surprised!"

I wasn't sure how I would get out of this one. As I'm driving, I look over and now Nick is touching up her lipstick, just beaming. She occasionally looks out the window to see where I'm taking her. A few very long minutes later, we pull up in front of the church, and she's looking completely confused, and I'm sweating bullets.

"Surprise!" I said, slightly nervous, slightly joking.

"What? What are we doing here? What's going on at church tonight?"

"It's group grief counseling. I signed you up!" I tried to make it sound as attractive as possible.

"GRIEF COUNSELING!!! WHAT?! Eric! Are you crazy?!"

Yeah, a little, I thought to myself.

"I thought you were taking me out to dinner! I am NOT going in there! I got all dressed up for GRIEF COUNSELING!" She starts crying and laughing at the same time.

Soon we're both laughing hysterically, and I confessed to her,

"When I saw you come out of the house all excited and dressed up, I knew I messed up! You didn't see how slow I started driving?!"

"I appreciate you, Hubby, but Boy, take me home."

There is no way to prepare your family (or yourself for that matter) in advance for the major life challenges that sometimes occur, I have learned that. But you can create an environment of love, stability, and support that will help them navigate those times just a little easier. And that matters. As dads, we can't prevent every unfortunate event from happening on the road of life that our family travels, but we can make sure that it's paved as smoothly as possible as we travel it. In our family, the consensus is that after surviving 2010, we can survive just about anything.

Lil' Eric, Big Things

In the fall of 2013, we sent Eric off to the University of Maryland. It had been a long road from his brain injury, and we tried to prepare him with the skills he would need to succeed in college. We were beyond proud. But by the spring of 2014, we were withdrawing him from Maryland as he had a GPA lower than anything I had ever seen. It was clear to me that he was doing everything *but* going to class. Eric was devastated, and *really* angry with us for taking what he believed to be extreme and unnecessary measures by pulling him out of school. I made him immediately enroll in the local community college and get a part-time job. He did everything we told him to do but still seemed to lack the drive he needed for success. My children have never been disrespectful, but Eric's moment of indifference *felt* disrespectful and caused me to grip him up more than once.

I was also concerned about the example Eric would set for his little sister. Taylor is seven years younger, and the two of them are so close that they'd may as well be twins. I can't tell you how many times she gave us the side-eye for being hard on her big brother during this time. But it was important to me that Taylor also understand that actions and inaction both have consequences. I could look at Eric and see that he was hurting because he thought I was disappointed in him, and I knew I had to find a way to help *him* fix this.

While we never stopped pushing him, I had to make sure that we were balancing our efforts with enough patience to allow Eric to grow up because that's really all he needed. I also reminded myself that while he had underperformed academically, he didn't do *half* the things I did while an undergraduate at Temple University, and for that I was grateful. And then one day, it clicked. Eric transferred to Cheyney University into the honor's program, on a full scholarship, soon after became a brother of Alpha Phi Alpha, Fraternity Incorporated, and graduated with honors. Baby Boy even taught elementary school for a year after graduating.

Conclusion

Several times this week my children called me on the phone; Eric greeting me with his trademark, "Dadd-dayyyyy!" and Taylor with her usual, "Hey Dad!" that always sounds like she's smiling from ear to ear. Eric is in Mexico right now attending the Black Entertainment and Sports Lawyers Association conference, and he's been calling me daily to tell me about it. He will be graduating from Florida A&M College of Law in just a few months. He plans to take the bar in NY, and ultimately become general counsel for a professional sports franchise. And my beautiful Baby Girl Taylor, well, she's a junior Kinesiology major at Hampton University on the pre-med track. She plans to become an orthopedic surgeon. There are no adequate words that would express my level of pride!

Eric and Taylor didn't come with a handbook, so being a Dad was the most important (and the longest) on-the-job training that I have ever had. Like many other parents, I've learned to place priority on my battles and make sure my responses are proportionate to the issues. I learned that there are times when one child needs more or less than the other, and I have had to adjust accordingly. I have learned for every "I love you" that we each give throughout the day, must also be demonstrated with time and undivided attention, and I view it as my role to set the example for that. Most importantly, I learned to allow my kids the space to tell me when I'm missing the mark so that I can fix it. There's no room for ego when you're serious about preparing two humans for this world.

My wife always jokes that we raised kids that are *way* better than we are, but she's actually right! I know for a fact that we hit the jackpot with these two humans! It is a gift to be able to have not only love but a genuine, deep admiration for the people that you have raised. There is a level of peace in knowing that the children you send out into the world will contribute to that world, and to the lives of those they encounter. And I can't wait to see it. I'm looking forward to every phase of my role as their father because just because my role may change, I know that the need for it won't.

You know, it's still crazy to me to hear these grown people calling *me* "Dad." It still gets to me. And yeah, it's *still* cool.

INTRODUCING KAREEM WASHINGTON

K areem Washington is a father to two girls, and a husband to his wife Kim Allen-Washington of over twenty years. Kareem and his family have lived in metro Atlanta for the past twelve years.

Kareem was born in Detroit, Michigan, and grew up in Lansing, Michigan. He played D1 basketball at Loyola Marymount University and Virginia Commonwealth University and graduated with a degree in Business Finance with honors. Kareem has worked in technology and digital advertising sales his entire twenty-five year professional work career.

Stacia Gowens et al.

BE SPECIAL: GIRL DAD BLESSING

I first want to start by thanking God and my two daughters Kamryn and Kendall for blessing me with being their Dad. I became a father for the first time in October 2004. Not just any dad, but a Girl Dad! Miss Kamryn forever changed my life's meaning. Anxiety, fear, a tremendous sense of responsibility, unimaginable joy, excitement, and happiness, but most of all, thanking God for the opportunity to be a Girl Dad. I'm the oldest of three boys, and ninety percent of my first and second cousins are male, so my childhood was very rough and tumble boy dominated. Besides my Mom, I had no real point of reference for living with, or around, girls. I always dreamt of being a father to girls, and my prayers were answered, not only once but twice when our second daughter Miss Kendall was born in October 2007.

I'm definitely far from perfect as a father, or husband, but more than anything my goal has always been to give our girls a foundation of love, self-motivation, inspiration, and affirmation to go out into this big world of opportunity knowing they have all the foundational tools to be what they want, to aspire daily, to...**Be Special!** That's my inspirational daily text message on our family text string in the morning when everyone says have a good day. My ending response is **#BeSpecial**. The meaning behind this phrase is to go ensure they go into every day, first being thankful to God for simply waking up and being healthy. Secondly, to know that they know are **AFFIRMED** as a Washington, having pride in where they come from and their family roots.

BE SPECIAL: In Sports

Many of the important life principles passed down to me from my childhood upbringing were life lessons taught through competitive sports. My wife and I have done the same with our girls. Both Kamryn and Kendall have played competitive travel club soccer since they were very little. Being a former college athlete myself, I try to inspire them as a parent sideline coach on **effort and competitiveness**. The principles of sports are the same regardless of what sport you play—prepare through practice and repetition, play hard, and give your best effort—everything else will take care of itself. My last pregame message as the girls get out of the car to play is: "**Play Hard, Have Fun, and Be Special!**" The lasting message I hope endures with them behind all that is, "You are not only playing for the team name on the front of your jersey to help them win (we are not one of those participation awards families, hey, just be happy to be out here). Rather, your goal for the game is to play to win, and be the best version of yourself for that game!

At the end of the day, this is really about playing the game of life, representing the name—your name—*on the back of your jersey*. After every game, before I give my post-game constructive critique (smile), I ask them:

- How do you think you did?
- What do you think you did well, what areas could you get better?
- Were you happy with your effort?
- What could you have done better to help your team win?
- Rank your play in that game on a scale from 1-10.

I believe that if you play with that level of passion and personal accountability, everything else will take care of itself.

BE SPECIAL: In Becoming a Citizen of the World

The greatest gift we've tried to share with our girls is self-love, cultural exploration, and appreciation through travel. Material things like a nice house, cars, clothes, and money are all great, but the most impactful and memorable life experiences we've tried to share with our girls have been our family trips. Our goal is to give them a curiosity and appreciation for cultures beyond the cushy metro Atlanta suburbia-blessed life they have grown up in. When and if they decide to have a significant other, or eventually get married, they can say to their potential partner, "you gotta come correct, my mom and daddy already gave me that travel experience."

Family Heritage

From a very early age, we've taken them on trips every year. Starting with knowing our family heritage, and where we come from, visiting their maternal and paternal family roots in New York City and Michigan, respectively. My parents still live in the same house on the Southside of Lansing that I grew up in. My girls always get a kick out of staying at Grandma and Papa's house and being able to sleep in the same small twin beds I slept in at their age. Watching them rummage through my old childhood toys, photo albums, reading or newspaper clippings from my high school basketball days, or listening as my parents tell them my childhood stories has been super special.

Conversely, my wife Kim is a first-generation *"Jamerican"* (my wife Kim was born in the Bronx, but both her parents were born and grew up in Jamaica and moved to the States as young adults). If you know anything about Jamaican culture, it is abundantly joyful and they take great pride in their homeland. My wife's family is no different. When we visit Long Island to see their grandparents, our girls also love sleeping in the bed Mommy grew up in at their age, trying on her old clothes, and developing a deeper understanding of their Mom's cultural family heritage of what it means to be Jamaican through family stories, amazing food, and family gatherings listening and dancing to old school reggae.

Black Girls Travel the World

Travel has always been a personal passion of mine that I wanted to develop an appreciation of with our girls. One of the ways to teach them to appreciate world cultures and diverse ethnicities is through travel. We've also been blessed to take them all over the U.S. for various family vacations and to attend out-of-state soccer tournaments. One of the biggest family trips to date occurred in the summer of 2018. We were able to combine their love of soccer with the opportunity to visit Europe where we visited Barcelona, Paris, and London all during the World Cup 2018 along with both of their grandmothers joining us on this memorable trip.

The first amazing city we visited on that trip was Barcelona. It is such a beautifully amazing place, I could live there. Both girls have a love of art. Kendall is an incredible drawer and painter (a God-given skill I wished I had developed more as a child). Barcelona is a very artsy-infused city with all the famous Antoni Gaudi inspired architecture and artwork throughout the city like the *La Sagrada Família* or Parc Güell. Kamryn is a budding foodie and loves to cook. Europe has some incredible, diverse opportunities to experience so many different foods. I would not be surprised if she became a famous chef as a career. Barcelona is a world-renowned soccer city with FC Barcelona aka Barca based there with some of the world's best soccer players. We visited Barca's soccer stadium, Camp Nou, one day on our trip, and the girls were so excited to walk on the ground where the likes of Messi and Neymar have played.

The next city on our European trip was Paris, "the city of love." Unbeknownst to us when pre-planning our itinerary, our Paris hotel was walking distance from the Moulin Rouge in the red-light district. Big OOPS! Not necessarily the type of "love" we wanted them to see at this young age, but we "made do" and pulled a few audibles to try and keep it G-rated! We made it a point to be done with our city exploration in Paris before sunset because the "block got hot and steamy" after dark in the Moulin Rouge neighborhood with adults doing what they do (think Las Vegas strip and South Beach combined at night). Paris is just a beautiful city with so much culture. Visiting The Eiffel Tower, Louvre Museum, Notre Dame Cathedral, and taking a boat down the famous Seine River was incredible even for me.

Our last stop was London. We took a three-hour train ride from Paris to London. London felt very familiar for them given the dominant language was English, and we felt a very similar vibe to NYC, just with much older historical city landmarks. One day, we were around Westminster and stumbled upon a celebration in the city, where the Royal family—yes, including the Queen—attended. Traveling with us was my mom and Kim's mom. Jamaican culture has a strong British influence, so being that close to the Royal family was a pretty cool experience for them too.

We timed our European trip during the 2018 World Cup. At each of our three city stops, the girls were lucky to get an authentic experience watching a high-level World Cup soccer game at a local bar with all the indescribable excitement and country pride that brings.

We've also been blessed to take them to Jamaica multiple times during their childhood to experience their mom's family roots. Living that beach and pool life insulated at a resort that caters to Americans is all good and fun, but we also aim to travel with a cultural appreciation purpose wherever we go and get outside of the cocoon of the resort experience by experiencing how the locals live. It could be anything from stopping off on the side of the road on our day trip drive from Montego Bay to Negril for authentic jerk chicken to splashing at the beach the locals go to down the road from Dunn's River in Montego Bay. Kim has family and friends throughout the island, so visiting a family friend's home or stopping at a restaurant owned by a family friend are just a few of the authentic travel experiences I hope they remember beyond just the all-inclusive resort experience.

We always make it a point to try and stay at really nice 4- and 5-star hotels or luxury resorts where possible (both my wife and I are kind of nice hotel snobs). My inner dad self, I also want to impress them so much now as teenagers, so that when they are young women having more mature dating experiences being courted by young men, they have a baseline of standards set by Dad. These young "thundercats" better come correct and ready to impress my girls! Not to impress for superficial vanity's sake, but that they put some real effort and personal investment into creating a meaningful travel experience. I still struggle with how to best talk to them about boys and how real to get, so I focus more on showing them by doing, and giving them experiences now, and trust those values translate into their adult relationship life.

BE SPECIAL: Representing for the Culture

Our girls are full-fledged teenagers now. Both are straight A student athletes, but I still struggle with how much to expose them with all the unrest and tension in the world today. My parents were very liberal with our upbringing and didn't shield us from much. My wife Kim grew up much more conservative and traditional, so we are constantly trying to find the right balance with our girls. Up until recent years, they've grown up in a world much more open to diversity, and their peer groups reflect that. All they've ever known was the "Hope" and "Change" of the Obama years. We even trekked from Atlanta to Washington, D.C. for Obama's second inauguration in 2012. They've been blessed to grow up in an era of not just tremendous progress with female empowerment, but Black female empowerment, with inspirations like Michelle Obama, Oprah, Venus and Serena Williams, and more recently, powerful young voices like Amanda Gorman, and countless other black women like Atlanta Mayor Keisha Lance Bottoms, who they got to meet in person.

My parents grew up during the civil rights movement of the 1960s, and they embedded a strong sense of self-love in me and my two brothers growing up. Fast forward to now, today's America presents some real backward-looking challenges we didn't have to deal with growing up. The current political climate in this country, the more explicit fear of the "*Other*" as America becomes browner, has made it even more of our priority for our girls to have unbending and unflinching love of self over anything. In 2016 with the election of 45, fueled by the rise of hate and racial animosity, it forced me to do some real soul searching about what it means to be a Black father of a Black daughter in today's America. How could this happen?

How could our neighbors in the mostly white Atlanta suburb neighborhood we live in, vote for and condone a man of his evil, con-man ilk, yet still think I'd be okay as a black father to allow my black daughter to play with their child and their family values as if this is okay or normal? **IT IS NOT.**

This continues to be in my thoughts and remains with me, even a year after the recent election of Joe Biden. To be honest, I still look at some of these folks in our neighborhood with a massive side-eye, as either complicit or active in that hate movement that was and is fueled by 45. I'm constantly reflecting back to the timeless Maya Angelou quote, *"when people show you who they are, believe them."*

The positive counterbalance to this has undeniably been the force of the Black Lives Matter (BLM) movement led by young people. Through the near-weekly police brutality stories like George Floyd, Breonna Taylor, and too many others who've lost their lives either as a result of police violence or some sort of strange "vigilante justice," it has been hard as a Black father to teach them life lessons of love, let alone deal with my own mental health. As much as we tried to discuss as a family and give meaning real-time to all that is happening, I feel like as a dad, I've learned as much from them and their resolve and self-initiated community activism over the last few years.

One example was a student-led BLM protest walk we attended as a family by the young people at Kamryn's private school. We protest marched with her peers through the streets of Buckhead (one of the most affluent communities in the city) to the Governor's mansion, listening to these young people sing chants of solidarity, empowerment, and activism. Most moving was witnessing such a diverse group of future leaders from all kinds of backgrounds come together, even during the summer days of the pandemic for a powerful and necessary cause.

Be Special: It's in Your Black Girl Magic DNA

The last and most important enduring life lesson we want them to embrace is Black Girl Magic! My wife Kim's female sister-friend group is deep and strong. These are women she's built lifelong bonds with going back to her college days to the present as women with families of their own, and leaders in their respective communities. It's one thing to have parents who share life lessons; it's another important element to have a village composed of so many powerful Black female Godmommies who can also inspire them, from a CEO of one of the largest nonprofits based in our hometown of Atlanta to leaders at premier education institutions, and business leaders who sit in C-suites. My wife's day job is Assistant Head of School at a premier private school here in Atlanta. During the stress and tragedy of the pandemic, the girls were able to gain a new level of appreciation and admiration for their mom, getting to see her firsthand help lead her school through the early days of the health crisis, all over Zoom.

Be Special: What I Know for Sure

What I've mostly learned about being a Black father to Black daughters is just as much as about teaching them as me learning and being adaptable to their ever-changing and evolving needs as young black women. I most admire our two girls for being so humble and treating everyone they interact with *earned* love and respect. So, I say to Miss Kamryn and Miss Kendall, thank you for allowing me to be your dad.

INTRODUCING RYAN L. BRAND

Ryan Brand is the founder and CEO of The Barber Boss, LLC, a consulting firm focused on bringing innovation and high-end solutions to clients who want to grow and scale their businesses. Mr. Brand brings over thirty years of expertise within the salon and barbering industry. His experience includes being a licensed cosmetologist, salon owner, trainer/instructor, and business consultant. Mr. Brand has earned an impeccable reputation in the hair business. After several years as a hair care professional and salon owner, he has now turned his talent and passion for the industry toward helping business owners and entrepreneurs take their businesses to the next level through his proprietary Barber Boss

Systems™. Mr. Brand also founded the nonprofit *Shears 2 Success*, where his goal is to help at-risk foster children by providing technical skills and vocational training. With insight from his own experience as a foster child, he is changing the narrative by helping youth become licensed hair care professionals and putting them on a path to owning their own business.

While Ryan Brand has had tremendous success professionally, his biggest source of pride is his family. Mr. Brand has been married for twenty-six years and has been fortunate to have four beautiful children. Mr. Brand's children have all graduated college and are pursuing their career interests and passions. By far Ryan's favorite activity is spending time with his family, but he also enjoys several outdoor hobbies in his spare time including traveling, kayaking, sailing, bowling, golfing, archery, and shooting sports.

IMPERFECTION: A FATHER'S SUPERPOWER

The key to becoming a caring, loving, nurturing, and supportive father is realizing your imperfection. I am grateful to have this opportunity to share my life experience as it relates to fatherhood. My approach to parenting is learning through experiences, particularly imperfect, challenging, life-altering ones that existed before and alongside my fatherhood journey. It excites me to share my perspective and experience by providing insight into my journey. Knowing this topic may be top of mind for existing and new fathers just beginning to navigate life's waters of lessons surrounding fatherhood, it's important to me to start with a humble mindset through my humble beginnings. My only expectation is that my sharing will speak to the young man who is now called father or to the "young man" who has been called father for more of his life than not. Nevertheless, may it speak to the young man inside us all searching for answers, strategy, and/or rare resonance to make sense of this thing called fatherhood.

When asked to contribute to this project, I was hesitant to take on such a responsibility. Fatherhood can be represented in so many ways. There are single fathers, married ones, fathers still courting and dating their partners, fathers who father from and with the support LGBTQ+ community, fathers who father across racial lines, non-biological fathers who father other's children, adoptive fathers, and too, the foster parent father, single mothers, uncles, grandparents, and coaches/community members who are assuming the father role and responsibility. Because I understand the magnitude and true bandwidth fathering requires, I do not take it lightly and therefore this undertaking seemed to be a Goliath-faced mirage, and I, David.

How Have You Been Successful at Being A Father?

My first response to this, always, is "I have been blessed, fortunate, and lucky in many respects, but successful, I have not." Parenting is the most difficult aspect of life. Forever evolving, continuously challenging, glaringly enlightening, and subsequently humbling, are just a few descriptions that speak to this journey. Perhaps there is no jury and they, then, are not "still out" on whether success has been achieved. But rather, the mere existence of becoming a father and breathing life into that cause, is what one may call "success." Its existence is a blessing I could not, and knowingly *did not,* orchestrate or mastermind on my own. There is a lot of destiny, God, and divine nature about it all that, lately, has led me to believe that willingly accepting this calling, being open to learning what it requires, *is* what it is all about. Those who champion fatherhood acknowledge their place in participating in a divine experience they were predestined for. This outlook is what I consider to be the foundation to any definition of success. It's what keeps me clear on what is mine to learn to handle, what is feasible, and what is above me. Speaking of above me, I didn't have to attempt fatherhood alone and had support in place that I had no part in curating. Yet, I had them (again, a nod to that destiny thing aforementioned). I not only had my father, but a father-in-law, multiple father figures, and an incredible wife who without hesitation was willing to learn to adapt and adjust on the fly as I was evolving and learning to be the best representation of a father figure. I would be remiss if I didn't offer a special thanks to my wife, my partner, and my best friend. You are truly an inspiration to me and our family, none of what we have accomplished as a family or as parents would have been as special and rewarding without you. I love you. Thank you to you all. Ironically, thank you to all my life's hardships and lessons that predate this support. I wouldn't have known how to utilize them had I not undergone what I share next. Thus, my mantra, answer, and word being, Imperfection is a father's superpower.

Imperfection: Make Way for Continuation

As mentioned earlier, fathers can show up in many ways. I was fortunate to have been adopted at six months old to my foster family. That is how "father" came to me. I was blessed, honored to call Ira Thomas Brand my father because he very literally _chose_ to call me son. There's a lesson in that. Sometimes it's just as simple as naming it and choosing to do it. However perfect or imperfect the "it" that you are facing may be, it is a necessary step and power for any beginning. My father's and mother's power in that decision would impact me immensely, shaping my foundations as a person, my influence, my outlook.

I grew up in a foster home. My parents were foster parents for many years and they functioned as such for most of my life until I was about fifteen years old. More specifically, they provided emergency housing for children in the foster care system who needed immediate temporary placement; that was how I found my family. I was abandoned at the hospital and left with no one, no family, no home to go to. My biological mother did not have what she felt she needed to care for a child, I was told later in life. I can applaud her for knowing her limitations, her circumstances, and attempting to give me a better chance at life. Therein lies another nugget of wisdom. This being my earliest influence, what most would see as disappointing, unfortunate, even inhumane, shaped me into being an individual who looks at the same set of circumstances and recalls themes of adaptation, honesty, and opportunity. In everything, I can't help but see the blessings. If one were to lean into this mindset a bit more when things seem troubling or bleak, my experience demonstrates that it ultimately leads to remaining open, bypassing the comfortable pit that despair can be, and getting to the problem-solving prompts like, "What can this lead to?" or "What does this set me up for that I couldn't have conceived on my own?" From these questions, start the small steps toward redemption and resolution. I share this part of me to give you context on how I was introduced to the concept of family and to demonstrate sometimes imperfection is all you have; it is on you to change it into the mindset your situation requires. That is not to say pain won't exist and that suppressing your feelings is advisable. Rather, it can be reshaped into expansive energy that continues you and your aims; sometimes that is survival, sometimes it is finding a home, sometimes it is much more complex, like something to do with fulfilling your role as a father. For me, that's the order in which my imperfections would resolve. I will forever be grateful to have someone step up in my life, who wasn't perfect, who loved and expressed love unconventionally, who already had four children of his own, but who found a little space in their heart for me. This imperfect path would pave the way for me to have a fighting chance at a future of my own.

After the gift of survival, there was growing up in my house and as a young kid, it was challenging. As I shared before, my parents had four biological children of their own and we had a revolving door of foster children coming and going. My adoptive siblings were much older than me and that became somewhat of a natural barrier to establishing a closeness between us as siblings. In retrospect, this isolation started my mental blueprint of ideas as small as, "one day, I want my children and family to be tight-knit." I became accustomed to meeting new kids. Some would stay for short periods; others would stay for much longer. I never quite knew if I should call them brothers and sisters or simply view them as friends. I quickly learned it was best to not get too attached because I never knew when I might wake up and find them gone. A revolving door of loneliness feeling outcasted, I was consumed with issues of abandonment, mistrust, and emptiness throughout the entirety of my childhood to young adult life. For many of the same reasons, I became hesitant to express feelings or demonstrate acts of love. Another contributing factor was that my parents, especially my father, had a hard time telling me he loved me. I never heard or very seldom heard the words, "I love you" during my time at home. While I have no doubt of their love for me, my parents were old school, and they tended to make it a priority to prepare you for life rather than hand it to you on a silver platter. With that comes tough love, hardship, struggle, confusion, instability, lack of assertiveness, and lack of life planning. Life merely becomes about struggle and survival. Me thinking that this was my biological family, and finding out as a fifteen-year-old boy that they were not, strangely affirmed the tumultuous waves of isolation; all the detachment, loneliness, and confusion actually made more sense. While I grappled with my existence, I also felt entirely responsible for it.

Not entirely belonging to any one person, place, or thing, I gravitated toward other father figures, football coaches, and my guidance counselor to fulfill the lacking inspiration, conversation, bonding, and quality time. Later in life, I finally realized that my struggle developed my perseverance as it pertains to cultivating necessary relationships. Many of us "hood kids" possess this fine art and are fluent in finding what we need in the world wherever we can. It is especially challenging to do this when what you need is human connection and relation, but luckily in building a makeshift panel of a "father," I know it to be possible. This once hurtful life positioning became another superpower and unknowingly, I filed in my mental Rolodex labeled "My Future" another demonstrative vow: "I will do all I can, if blessed to have children, to ensure they feel love, support, acceptance, and a sense of belonging."

The Inspiration

As a young father at the age of twenty-two, I was not prepared for what life and fatherhood had in store for me. All I knew was that I was determined to do things _completely_ opposite of the way my parents did. Because I associated my parents' parenting to struggle, lack of communication, and most importantly a lack of expressions of love and caring, I was hell-bent on showing love, always kissing my kids before bed, supporting them in every way I thought a father should, disciplining them differently, allowing them to be expressive, and encouraging them to share their feelings (well, sometimes). It wasn't until later in my life that I came to have a newfound appreciation for how my father did the very best that he knew that was based on his upbringing, his influences, his role models (or lack of), and learning how to navigate an orphan who he had agreed to parent and prepare for the world that would be full of questions, uncertainties, disappointment, inconsistencies, and unanswered questions. He did the absolute best he could, and I am extremely grateful for him having the foresight and the awareness to raise me with strength, resiliency, love, passion, commitment, fearlessness, and tough skin.

You see, we often strive or innately develop skills based on needs, wants, and desires. Many see the "lack of" as disappointing, I see it as a blessing. The question is, did my father see it the same way? Was he intentional in how he prepared me not to be spoiled, to develop a desire to acquire the things I didn't have, and develop a work ethic and grit to go after my heart's wildest dreams, to raise my family with some of the lessons he instilled in me? I would say yes, yes, and yes. I wish as a young father I knew then what I now know. Therefore, after several conversations, mainly with myself, about whether I should participate in writing this chapter or if I truly had something that would help another father, the answer became much clearer to me. I am participating to offer my experience in hopes that my story finds its way to listening ears in need of guidance, advice, and familiarity that will be a blessing to them and their family.

It Takes a Village

It truly takes a village to raise a child. No matter what your village looks like, it is important to seek advice, guidance, perspective, and support when raising your children. I will tell you that without the help and support of my family, both immediate and extended, raising my children would have been much more difficult. As a young father, there was so much to learn, and without the counsel and support of those that had experience raising a family, I can honestly say I would have been lost. As I mentioned earlier, my mother was a foster care mother for many years, so taking care of children was what she was best at. She was so instrumental in helping me understand the importance of schedules, regimen, discipline, and accountability. An important parenting principle that my mother demonstrated when I was at an early age is the power of loving your child, but equally holding them accountable. My mother would love me unconditionally, but she did not spare the rod. If I did something that warranted me being held accountable, she always would follow through and make it a teachable moment. She knew that this would be critical to me as I became a young adult and had to make decisions on my own. Understanding that decisions could potentially have consequences, some more consequential than others, it was *imperative* that I understood how to weigh my decision and understand the effects of my actions. I can honestly say, this was one of the most important life lessons that I carried with me into parenting my children.

Loving your children through the bumps in the road while teaching them that accountability for their actions is a critical life lesson that will stick with them for their entire lives. As I reflect on the many lessons that my village taught me, it is clear now that most of the parenting was focused on building life skills that would have a profound impact on adulthood. My in-laws were amazingly supportive and were always willing to step in and help no matter the circumstances. We could always count on them to help fill the gaps due to our busy work and school commitments. That kind of spirit has been very influential in my parenting of my children. With few questions, I learned to truly understand what it means to drop everything and be present, no matter the circumstances. As a parent, you show up and show support. What's important is for my children to know that under any circumstances both good and bad, they can count on me to be there. My wife and I were extremely blessed to have parents and other family members that we could count on to be there if we needed them no matter the circumstances. That feeling of unconditional support is incredibly comforting and reassuring. Not every family is structured to show up the same. A parent must seek to build a village with vital support lines to help ease the burdens and challenges that life will certainly throw your way.

My advice to a young parent is to be thoughtful and consider the impact and desired outcomes as you begin to build pillars of discipline, teachings, life lessons, and be extremely thoughtful of how it may prepare your child for life's many challenges as well as opportunities.

Imagination Means "Dare to Be Different"

My father-in-law instilled in both of his daughters the idea of daring to be different. When my wife and I were married in 1995, this became something I heard at most family gatherings along with discussions my wife and I would have as we were trying to understand what was important to instill in our children for their benefit and to fulfill this idea that each generation should be better positioned to raise a family and achieve individual goals and aspirations. This concept was not quite as clear to me before getting married. My parents wanted me desperately to go to college to better myself and in their own way, this was their plan to help lift our family unit to higher education and open the doors to more opportunities not only for myself but my future family. My wife's parents illuminated the importance of being mindful and intentional about how we plan and execute career pathways that will not only be fulfilling individually, but more importantly, uplift the family unit. My father-in-law truly has sacrificed so much to ensure that his daughters had the required stability, educational foundation, and confidence in themselves. The family name matters and should be honored, respected, and elevated for future generations to be able to take full advantage of the sacrifices endured by their families so that they could have more opportunities to fulfill dreams, goals, and live better lives than the previous generations.

Daring to be different was the motto. I fell in love with this idea and subscribed to the importance of instilling this into our children. Every chance my wife and I had to discuss the future, life planning, setting goals, matriculating through grade school, we would echo my father in-laws' message of daring to be different in everything you do. Pushing yourself to be different requires hard work, commitment, extra attention to detail, creative thought, strategy, focus, and faith. It can be much easier to follow the norm, commit to a blueprint that has worked out every detail, has all the answers to challenges and obstacles. My father-in-law knew that this approach would create complacency, potentially a lackluster career, and a life lacking passion and purpose. This concept is brilliant to me, and I believe that each child deserves the opportunity to be expressive and dare to be different in all they seek to do.

The life and career skills that were innately embedded in my wife as a young girl have been the solid foundation that has helped her build an amazing career, become an awesome mother, live a life filled with purpose, passion, fearlessness, and a commitment to challenge the boundaries by continually daring to be different. As a father, I had to become very imaginative and have faith in something I could not see, nor had ever seen before, in my life. I knew I had arrived at the imaginative destination when a man like from where I came from, with a very hard-nosed, prideful, "man's man" father, who was as "grin and bear it" as they come, an athlete, a young man on his own, an entrepreneur...defied typical household gender roles and welcomed the responsibility of being my kid's caregiver while my wife worked for pivotal portions of our life. For the first time as a father, I bet on difference being better than what I knew or was comfortable with. And because of it, things have turned out better for my kids than I could have ever masterminded.

Anyone who feels like they haven't been afforded their opportunity can do this because it encourages you to look at the difference between yourself and where you'd like to be, act on it with courage, and to not do only what you know, but what you need to know now. I was already daring to be different from my imperfect life by just trusting and trying what my new loved ones had shared.

My wife and I began to live by this motto, "Dare to be different". When my children began grade school, daring to be different was top of mind in just about every approach to whatever the interest was. From academics to sports and or hobbies, we approached and applied this principle knowingly to instill hard work, preparedness, and impact at an early age. We always sought out and adopted the idea that daring to be different would require extra hours, extra practice, additional resources, and a level of commitment to see it through. Not fully knowing how this approach would play a vital role in our children's success as they grew up and now as young adults, we implemented it anyway. No matter the focus or the interest at the time, we only had one approach. Try to be your very best and learn to identify how having a "daring to be different" approach will not only push you towards being your absolute best and living up to your true potential, but it will also never leave you satisfied. Daring to be different often will keep you up at night trying to solve problems and create new strategies and approaches when seeking to live each day better than the last.

One of the most powerful outcomes that a parent could hope for when encouraging their children to dare to be different is that they would find new ways to solve problems, innovate, and explore to impact the change they want to see in themselves, others, and the world. That ultimately, they will find themselves living a life that is filled with passion, reward, optimism, and happiness. I believe that applying the "daring to be different" approach as a young father especially, helps maintain the imagination and vulnerability that he possessed in his youth and allows him to marry it with his newfound capability and resource as a man and provider. This solicits new opportunities that will bring more to his family, his cause, and his family's honor.

This dare was a truth-AND-dare for me. I had to be honest and accept my imperfections, set my pride aside, and get real about how different I wanted things to be. From there, the dare is being willing to imagine more. Get this, imperfection can be infinitely different, can it not?

Everything is Perfect

I cannot say whether I have been definitively successful at being a father or not, as much as I can talk about where my biggest areas of growth, redemption, and learning have come from. Imperfection has provided me with the gift of remaining open and hungry for life. It fueled my introspection and personal investigations as to why and how parenting is a stylistic choice for the right now and tomorrow. And finally, it has kept me young because I am compelled to continue imagining and reimagining as I grow alongside my kids. **Open, introspective**, and **imaginative** are the attributes I have embodied as a father, through the inevitable imperfection we all face. Consider what you might shape-shift the imperfection around you into. Alice Walker once said, "In nature, nothing is perfect, and everything is perfect. Trees can be contorted, bent in weird ways, and they're still beautiful."

There is nothing more natural than being a father, than life continuing. As fathers, as the builders of our families, our communities, and the world, as we know it, we ought not to limit ourselves to the finite confines of perfection, but rather take heed to what Ms. Walker realizes, that there is infinite, boundless power and beauty in imperfection. How will you choose to see it? My measure of the job I've done with this tall task is not based on what my kids choose to do with their lives, how much money they make, or how much they become what I want them to. The truest measure is much bigger than that. It's in them trusting I am here, willing to be reflective and solution-oriented, and thinking of all their future possibilities. From there, anything is possible. From there, the future is always bright. Success, then, is not a quantifiable goal but a byproduct of life, all its imperfections included.

I am not a perfect father, yet somehow, I am. My sincerest advice is to have an open mind, be nonconforming (you know, dare to be different), expect challenges, be vulnerable, ask for help, and continue to ask forgiveness from your children for allowing you the space, imperfection, understanding, and patience that allows you to learn how to become a better father as we all grow and experience this thing called life together.

INTRODUCING DEMIAS PEGUES

D emias Pegues was born and raised in the small town of Elkhart, Indiana. He lived with his mother and older brother and, although his father was local, was raised by his mother. Demias grew up in a close community surrounded by many family members and friends.

After graduating from high school, Demias attended Purdue University and received his B.S. in Engineering. There he met his wife of over twenty-eight years, Kathy-Ann. Demias went on to work at a family-owned business and for General Motors before attending Indiana University to receive his Master's in Business. Since completing graduate school, Demias has worked in retail, telecommunications, and healthcare. He is currently the Chief Operating Officer for Great Lakes Dental Partners, a Dental Services Organization serving Chicagoland and Northwest Indiana.

Kathy-Ann and Demias have three wonderful children: Jamila, Nia, and Elijah (Eli). Jamila has her undergraduate degree from Princeton University and her PhD in Astrophysics from Harvard. She currently lives in Baltimore, Maryland. Nia is a sophomore at Oberlin College in Ohio, and Eli is a senior in high school. For fun, the family enjoys traveling and attending events together. They also have movie nights when they are all together.

A CHALLENGE: TO GIVE YOUR LIFE

My Story

At the time I am writing this, I am a healthy, nearly-fifty-year-old Black male, I have a B.S. in Engineering and an M.B.A, I am a Chief Operating Officer of a small and growing company, and—most importantly—I am on my twenty-eighth year of marriage to my beautiful wife, and we have three adult children together. Our oldest child is the first Black female to graduate from Harvard University with a Ph.D. in Astrophysics, our middle daughter is a sophomore at Oberlin College in Ohio, and our youngest son is a senior in high school and is very much college bound. By the grace of God, they are all doing well and making their own way in the world. These are all things that I am truly proud of and consider blessings. They are also things that, given my background and story, were statistically not likely. Las Vegas would have considered them long shots.

My mom and dad got divorced when I was a baby, so I don't have any memories of them together. My mom remarried a couple of times and had long-term boyfriends, but those men were not really with her to raise her kids, so I had mostly a superficial relationship with them. Plus, some of them were awful people. The bottom line is that I did not learn how to be a father from someone in my home. My wife's story is similar to mine. Her mom and dad were never together, and, in fact, she never really knew her father. Tragically, several years back, her father died suddenly, right when she was getting to know him.

Having few or distant male role models in my life impacted me at a young age. I knew very early on in life that, if I ever had kids, I would be an everyday presence in their lives. I had friends that had active, positive male role models, and I could see that it mattered. From our discussions and through my observations, I knew they were getting advice, support, and guidance that I was not getting. Someone was rebounding for them when they practiced their jumpshots at the neighborhood court, while I was getting my own rebounds. I imagined my future kids and determined that I would be there for them, no matter what. At the time, it all sounded easy enough—once you have kids, just be there every day. In reality, however, life taught me that "being there" was easier said than done. We are not parents in a vacuum. We are parents with other people involved in our children's lives and actively have to manage relationships, marriages, personal goals, careers, and other family matters. It can all be difficult to navigate, stressful, and all-consuming. So, honestly, I really do understand why some fathers, like mine and my wife's, end up not being around their kids when they grow up. No judgment; I get it, but I was resolved not to BE it.

My wife and I got married in college while we were at Purdue University, and we decided to have a child right away. We were two young people in college without a strong marital support network, and we decided to get married and have a child. Not the best or most well thought-through idea we have ever had. Our naivety, lack of support, and inability to solve even small problems led to our getting divorced after only three years of marriage. Following our divorce, we were off and on as a couple. We tried to stay together, but would end up breaking up, and we were rarely on the same page at the same time.

Then, after four years of being divorced and living apart, I learned an important life lesson. I learned the value of being honest with myself. I was miserable without my wife, and I was miserable being away from our daughter. Not that I stopped living, I didn't. However, there were massive holes in my life and in my spirit, and I could not fill them. That was the truth. And, once I was really honest with myself, the fact that my family was not together was my issue to resolve. It was a ball bouncing around that I had dropped, and I knew I needed to pick up and make my family whole again. All marriages are different but, in ours, it was my role to protect us, and I had failed to protect us from ourselves. We were not together and that was on me.

So, I stopped lying to myself, picked up the phone, called my then ex-wife, and was honest with her. I told her that I was miserable without her and that, if she would have me back, we would never divorce again. As a matter of fact, I asked her to commit to taking the "d" word off the table as an option for "solving problems." It was a simple concept: if the d-word was not an option, then all our other options would require us to work it out: counseling, retreat to different parts of the house, take a very long walk, compromise, agree to disagree. I am not saying that the d-word did not come up after we remarried; it did. However, we were never close to calling a lawyer. Or at least I wasn't! My grandmother used to tell me, "It takes two to tango and two to argue. If you are not arguing back, then you are not in an argument." Like I said, it was my job to keep us together, and I thought of this responsibility often and took it seriously. It is who I am, so I still do!

This was the second life lesson that I learned from marriage. I learned the very real power and gravity of true commitment to a person, a belief, or an idea. My wife and I agreed that the d-word was not an option but, secretly, I had committed to making the d-word cease to exist. I was all in. If she decided on the d-word, then I would of course honor her wishes. But for me, I would never consider it again. I was prepared to make sacrifices to remain together and that trumped all else. Things like who won the last argument, how we aged physically, or even how often we had sex became less important compared to my commitment to her. In the grand scheme, most things became small bumps in the road or passing storms on the path to better days. But I truly committed to the journey and the work it requires. Marriage is definitely not easy; it is for sure not impossible; it is just hard. So now, when my wife and I hit rough spots and our communication starts to break down, we seek counseling from a trained, licensed marriage counselor. In other words, when our communication—or anything else—is "sick," we go see a doctor that can help us get back on track. Counseling has helped me learn how to be a better husband.

My Challenge to You

So, what does this have to do with fatherhood? It's simple: what was best for my child at the time I divorced my wife, was for me to stay committed to my marriage. Despite loving my wife and my child, I walked out on them. The road became bumpy and then really, really bumpy, and I left. The storm came and I ran for shelter elsewhere. I split, I ran, and I left my wife to do the hard work of everyday parenting. I walked out on my wife, and I walked out on our daughter. Almost thirty years later, it hurts to admit this, but I am just being honest—with myself and with you. Would my daughter be the first Black female astrophysicist from Harvard if I never came back? Maybe—my wife is an extraordinary mother and would have probably figured it out. Thankfully, I will never know the answer to that question.

Men, both current and future fathers, I have a challenge for you: give your life to your children. Have you ever said or thought that you would give your life for your child? Take a bullet or run into a burning building to save her even if the chances were you would not make it? I have, and I meant it.

Thus, I challenge you to give <u>your life to your children</u>. Not your death, as in take a bullet, but your life, as in give your time, energy, resources, commitment. Don't just give your intangible love from a distance but, rather, give your tangible, concrete presence and availability. Be at the plays and the games. Be by their side during the heartbreaks and the late-night study sessions. Support them through both their good and bad decisions. <u>Be there for your child</u> and, yes, their mother. <u>Figure it out; sacrifice</u>. Let the bullet you take be your unwavering commitment to them; let the fire you rush into be your ever-present availability. <u>Put it all on the line</u> to be there and, when you turn fifty, I promise you will not regret it.

Stacia Gowens et al.

INTRODUCING KEVIN WHITE

Kevin White is the middle child of nine and knows the phrase "the struggle is real" all too well. He was born in Indianapolis, Indiana and raised in College Park, Georgia. As a child, Kevin lacked confidence and took a lot of things personally. Instead of acting out in a negative way, his personal outlet was music and dancing. Growing up, his favorite performer was Michael Jackson. He always dreamed of being on stage and performing in front of large audiences. Through hard work and dedication, his dreams came true. Kevin's dancing talent took him to the stages of the Grammys, BET

Awards, VMA's, Billboard Music Awards, VH1 Fashion Awards, Soul Train Music Awards and the world famous Apollo Theater. Kevin performed with many chart-topping artists such as TLC and Monica, just to name a few.

Eventually Kevin transitioned from the big stage to the corporate stage. Kevin became a dynamic sales leader and was globally recognized and recruited to help grow a call center in Cairo, Egypt. There, he spent three years training and recruiting over 1,000 Egyptian college students. Today Kevin is the Lead Corporate Sales Trainer at a top software company in the USA, Australia, and Canada. He is a business and life coach, mentor, certified behavioral practitioner, and motivational speaker.

He is also a founding partner of Vanguardian Global—a business that specializes in event production, talent booking, consulting and business coaching. Kevin has always been recognized as a passionate teacher paired with a huge dose of servant leadership. No matter what title or role he plays to the world, his greatest accomplishment is being a supportive husband and a loving father of two amazing children.

FAMILY CONNECTION

As I write this, it's 2021 and I am a forty-nine-year-old man. Sometimes, I marvel at how I got here. You see, I come from a large family with two very hard-working parents. Life was by no means easy, and even though mom and dad did everything they could for us, it was still tough. When I was in third grade, we moved to College Park, Georgia. The move was scary, but getting away from the snow was welcomed. Even though the state had changed, the scenery remained the same. During this time we moved a lot and had the typical problems any large family in the hood would have. But one thing was very clear—we always had a family connection. My dad would sit us down and talk to us about life and how he grew up in deep Mississippi. He would always say, "If someone messed with one of y'all, they messed with all of y'all! Protect each other." And that's what we did. As we got older, the connection only got stronger.

Shortly after graduating high school, I met a girl that eventually changed my life forever. At the time I didn't see her as my wife, I saw her as my best friend. Tasha saw beyond all my childhood insecurities and looked at me as the man I would one day become. At the time neither one of us could articulate our feelings very well, but we knew there was something special happening between us. Tasha and I went from being friends to lovers to married within a five-year span. In 1995, Tasha decided to travel out west to be closer to her family. In my mind, I didn't see this being anything permanent. At least not until month two of her being away. I asked her, "when are you coming home?" She replied, "I am home, and I have no plans on coming back…" I was like, Wait a minute! I immediately booked a flight to Las

Vegas with all intentions of convincing Tasha to come back to Atlanta with me. Once I got there, I saw opportunities that I didn't see in Atlanta. Needless to say, love won this round and Las Vegas became my new home.

Since then, I've toured the world with award-winning artists and performed on multiple award shows. I touched the pyramids of Egypt and met some of the most passionate people on the planet. As amazing as that all sounds, there is nothing that can compare to being a dad to my two wonderful children, Jaelin and KJ (Kevin Jr.). They have taught me so much as a human, as a father, and as a friend. I didn't always have a lot, or at least that's what I thought. It turns out I had everything I needed. Let's rap a taste, and allow me to share with you how a few conversations changed my perspective and how a lasting connection to your child doesn't start with "Goo, goo, gaa, gaa."

My Baby Bear

It's one thing to find out you're having a baby, but, for me, when I found out the gender of my firstborn child, my imagination ran wild. I was twenty-four years old and on tour with one of the top female R&B artists, Monica, at the time. We were in Atlanta rehearsing and I was staying at my brother's place while in town. At 6:00 am on March 1st, my sister-in-law woke me up saying "Tasha is on the phone." I was confused because I didn't understand why she didn't call me directly. But she had, I was just knocked out. When I said hello, Tasha said "my water broke and I'm on my way to the hospital". I told her to stop playing and then heard my mother-in-law in the background saying, "get here, Kevin." My heart sank and I got so nervous. At that time, there was no Zoom or FaceTime, so I couldn't see her. All I knew was I needed to get home!

I booked a flight, packed all my stuff, and was headed home. There were so many new dad questions running through my head; "What was meeting her for the first time going to be like?" I wanted to be there when she took her first breath, but I wasn't. Who's going to judge me for working and not being there? How will I explain to her that I wasn't the first face she saw? I was already imagining what school functions would be like. Her first dance recital, doing science fair projects with her. Sitting at college graduation, beaming with pride. I was so nervous and didn't want to make any mistakes, but I also knew there is no rule book when it comes to parenting, so inevitably, I would. Where was I going to start?

I wanted to give my baby everything I didn't have growing up, and that was where I stopped. I didn't think about her falling in love or getting married. Not MY baby girl! No one was going to be good enough. I didn't think about it until it was too late. I firmly believe in the power of connection and that this is a story that every father that has a "baby girl" can relate to.

Being a professional dancer, I was on tour, and I would be in and out of town for work. I remember coming home from a trip and the house was full of family and friends. Music was going and everyone was laughing, talking. Jaelin was about two years old at the time and was drinking a glass of water. I saw her across the room choking. I didn't panic because I felt like if she had seen me panic, she would have panicked. I picked her up and took her into another room. I just kept talking to her while gently patting her on the back until she was okay. With tears in her eyes, she just looked at me. I asked her if she was okay and she nodded her head yes. I then asked her if she was scared, and she nodded her head yes. At that time, I just looked into her big brown eyes and said, "don't worry, daddy will always be here to protect you." She grabbed my neck and hugged me so hard that I could hardly breathe. My heart swelled. THIS was the moment I became her hero.

That was the moment our connection happened. She knew dad had her back and she was going to run full speed after whatever she wanted. During the times I was on tour, I often felt like I was missing the opportunity to connect with my baby girl, but when I was home, it was all us. She and I would do everything together. From the barbershop to dance practice she was always with dad. I felt like we were ready to take on the world, but there was one little issue…Little Boys!

Question: When was the moment you made that special connection to your child and they saw you as their protector, hero, or comforter? What was the situation and how did it make you feel? Is there a lesson in that moment that you could share with other fathers to help them establish a connection with their child?

*Creating that Family Connection" now can help strengthen the bond between you and your child for the more challenging years ahead.

I Don't Like Little Boys

I don't like little boys. Let's just get that out right now! I recall a time when I had to pick Jaelin up from pre-K. The teacher greeted me at the front and asked me to speak to her in private. As I sat down, I could tell she was uncomfortable. So I asked, "what's going on?" She said she was a little uncomfortable sharing what she was about to share with me because she didn't know what my reaction would be. At this point, I stood up and said, "where's my daughter?" She finally told me that a boy kissed my Jaelin. SAY WHAT? I said okay, well, can I talk to this little boy? She said no, and I asked, "who is he?" She said she couldn't tell me, but she would be having a conversation with his parents as well.

This situation caused me to flashback to when I learned that our firstborn child would be a girl and I immediately knew that I was going to have an issue with little boys. My thinking was, little boys would be a distraction so they were not going to be allowed in her life. Period! No boys! This would ensure we had noooo problems! So, when I heard about this kissing incident, I didn't hear one word about the need for discretion from the teacher, I had an immediate issue and I was going to solve it—my way. I didn't care if the little boy was only four years

126

old. In my mind, he crossed the line, and he would pay! When I went into the classroom to get my baby girl, I mean mugged every little boy in that room. They all just looked at me with smiles on their faces, not knowing I was on the hunt. When I saw Jaelin, she ran up to me and gave me a big hug. I asked how her day was. She said it was good and I took her for ice cream like I always did. We didn't talk about what happened at all.

Once we got home, I told Tasha what happened and she said, "things happen and although it was inappropriate, there is not a damn thing you can do to that little boy. Yes," she continued, "that includes waiting for him after school on the playground." Nonetheless, our responsibility was to communicate with Jaelin and to make sure she knew that was inappropriate behavior at this age without embarrassing her. For me, it was inappropriate at any age; remember, NO BOYS, PERIOD! So when Tasha and I sat down with Jaelin, we tried to make it a very casual conversation. This was going to be hard. The last thing I wanted was to damage the connection we had established with Jaelin. As we explained that she had done nothing wrong, but this was not appropriate for a young lady her age. I could see in her eyes that she was sad. She felt like she let us down and I couldn't leave our conversation like that. This is when communication and connection matter most. I just smiled and said, "Let me ask you a question. Have you ever let us down or disappointed us?" She responded quietly, "no." I said, "I know, you could never disappoint us. Besides, all of your kisses are for daddy!" She laughed and gave me a big hug.

From that point on, I was on "High Alert!" Middle school and high school were no different. We didn't have any more incidents, and I definitely wasn't a fan of Jaelin dating. But Tasha convinced me that she was mature enough to handle it, and she wasn't going to cross any lines to worry us.

Trust Your Teaching

From time to time, I needed to remind myself that I just needed to trust that everything I had taught her over the years and the lessons she learned would help in her decision-making as she became a young woman. When I look back on it, it was never Jaelin that I had the trust issues with, it was the boys I didn't trust. For most daughters, their first love is their father. Whether it's what they see when dad loves and respects their mom or those comforting conversations only a father can have with his baby girl. The bottom line, I wanted Jaelin to always feel like her dad is here and will always be her protector no matter what. These were the qualities I wanted her to see in the man she would call her own. I made sure to bring her roses for every graduation from pre-K to college because I was setting a standard for the qualities in a future mate that Jaelin would recognize as worthy of her.

Question: Think of a time when you had to have a tough conversation with your child. How did it go? Would you do something different? What advice would you give a parent that has to have a tough conversation with their child but doesn't want to push them away or ruin their connection?

The hardest part for me was to trust in what I had taught her. You don't always have to come from a place of authority and discipline. Have a conversation with her/him and make them understand and agree to whatever punishment is coming. Even if it's a hug.

No, I Wasn't Ready!

To borrow a popular quip from Kevin Hart, "No, I wasn't ready!" And still, it happened—what I could never bring myself to imagine, happened. My daughter's wedding day. Fathers, you might want to grab a drink or light a cigar while I share this. There is nothing conventional about this part of the story.

July 6, 2018. Jaelin and her fiancé James, who was a long-time boyfriend, decided they wanted to get married. Now I will say, James was very proper in his approach. He came to me and asked for my blessings to be engaged, but that was it. I wasn't quite ready to approve the marriage. James seemed to understand how I felt about it. I wanted to get to know them as a couple first before they became a married couple. I felt like I would be able to mentor and build on my relationship with my future son-in-law during their engagement, as well as keep my eyes open for red flags. To me, there was no need to rush into this and James hadn't met her four uncles in Atlanta yet. I wanted their discerning eyes on the young man too! Once he met them, we would see if he still felt the same way about marrying my baby girl. Though he had been around the family for a long time, I wasn't convinced he was *the one*, so I was definitely tough on him. In my humble opinion, and after twenty-five years of marriage myself, I believe marriage is the hardest job on the planet. You have to share responsibilities, deal with mood swings, and meet challenges from every direction. So yeah, I was tough on the young man, just like a good father should be. I didn't even call the young man by his real name. KJ and I made up names like Jerome and Jimmy, just to mess with him. And he would just smile and answer respectfully. At that point, he started growing on me. Come to think of it, I don't think I started calling him James until they got engaged.

I remember waking up to my wife saying, "calm down, calm down, it's okay." It was Jaelin and she sounded like she was crying. I immediately got pissed! She was balling uncontrollably and I couldn't hear why. My wife just said, "it's okay, just tell me what happened". Now I'm about to get my gun(s). She stopped sobbing just long enough to tell us that she and James went downtown to the courthouse and got married the night before. *WHAT?!* Now Jerome was really going to get it. I told him good, I was okay with the engagement, but I was not ready for marriage! (Like I was the one getting married.) They took it too far and I felt taken advantage of. I was all in my feelings and was two minutes from taking out all the anger from pre-K years ago on James. He was going back to Jerome for good in my book.

While I was getting dressed and about to go hunt Jerome, down my wife said "I guess that's karma," with a smirk on her face. I said, "what are you talking about, and why are you smirking?" And then it hit me—over twenty-three years ago we did the same thing. We eloped and told our parents afterward. Is this what our parents felt way back then? Man, I would give anything to have a conversation with my Pop and Big L, the nickname for my father-in-law, right now. But I'm sure they're both looking down on us and laughing.

Well, what was done was done—although I still had my feelings about it, I was going to make sure that Jaelin knew that being married was not something you could do part-time. James was her husband and partner and although I will always be her dad, she was no longer going to be on my medical insurance. He was going to pay her phone bill and put gas in her car.

Passing the Torch Was Hard

This was really hard for me. I was very confident in the woman my daughter had become, but realizing it was time to step aside and allow another man to take care of her was tough. Meanwhile, my wife, who also felt a lot of the same feelings, seemed to be focused on Jaelin having a traditional wedding. I wasn't sure if that was for her or my daughter because it really made no sense to me why I needed to pay for something that had already happened (still in my feelings as you can see). But, Jaelin was still daddy's little girl with the key to my heart. By the time she finished working her magic on me, I was all in. So a year later, our family hosted Jaelin and James' wedding. I will say it took every bit of that year for me to prepare, considering I was still trying to comprehend that my daughter was someone's wife. I told y'all I didn't like little boys, and with tears in our eyes while I walked her down the aisle, she said "don't cry or I'm going to cry," but it was way too late for that. I reached out to shake James' hand and he gave me a bear hug. I simply told him to take care of my baby girl and he said, "I will." I took my seat, wiped my eyes, and my wife said, "it's okay, baby.

She's in good hands." Not what I *wanted* to hear, but what I *needed* to hear, so shout out to the wives who always know just what to say to support their husbands! Right at that moment, one person came to mind—KJ. Where is he and how is he taking this? KJ was fifteen at the time. When I spotted him, he had tears in his eyes as well.

Question: Have you ever had to step back and let your child handle a situation on their own? How did it make you feel? Did you trust in the teachings you instilled? What advice would you give a father facing a tough decision like letting another man take care of his daughter?

Trusting that this was the right decision for her was tough because I know what is good for her! Or so I thought. How could I say that when what I wanted could potentially make her unhappy? Believe in what you instilled, and be there to catch them if they fall.

The Arrival of Prince Kareem

There was a time after Jaelin was born when my wife said, "I don't think I want any more children." When I asked why, she replied, "because I don't think I could love another child as much as I love Jaelin." I thought that was deep, but I came from a family of nine and thought that if my mother ever thought that way I wouldn't be here right now. But I did get it, the love I was feeling for this little girl was something I had never felt before in my life. This love was a different kind of love. How could I give this kind of love again? Well, I needed to figure it out because eight years later almost to the actual day, our second child, our boy, Kevin Kareem White, affectionately known as KJ, was born March 2nd, eight years and one day after his sister. How we timed that, I don't know. Jaelin was adamant about not sharing her birthday with her little brother. Even though she was excited to meet him, she was not going to change her mind.

At this point in my life, I was a Sr. Sales Manager living abroad in Cairo, Egypt. That's how KJ got his middle name, Kareem. All of my

Egyptian friends in Cairo gave me the nickname "Kareem." They said it meant generous and kind. During my time abroad, I met a lot of amazing people and made some really great friends, so, when KJ was born, it was a no-brainer to make it an official name our family revered. He would be "Prince Kareem." He was such a happy baby. Even when I took him to our office in Cairo, all of the Egyptians gave him so much love and attention and he never cried once. He only laughed and smiled not knowing these were the very people who gave him his middle name. Or maybe he did know. When KJ was around seven years old, he told Tasha and me that he picked us as his parents when in heaven (I know, that's heavy).

We spent three years in Cairo before returning to the States, and one thing I can tell you for sure, the weather there is always beautiful. We lived on a golf course in a house that was affectionately known by all the team as "The Pink House." It was a house straight off of *MTV Cribs*. Swimming pool, game room, multiple kitchens, and tons of rooms. It was a great time.

As my time in Cairo was coming to an end, Tasha and the children went home first. They went to her grandparents' house in Michigan to spend some time with them so they could see their great-grandson for the first time in the flesh. Tasha and I have always been a bit unconventional and didn't live life the way many others thought we should. We did things our way, which was not always received by our families so well. As a young father, everyone is going to offer advice on how to raise your kid(s), and my advice is, "Listen to understand, not to respond." You don't know what you don't know. Just like anything else, keep the good, let the bad go, and try not to take it personally. One piece of advice I decided to keep is from a conversation I had with Tasha's grandfather, "Papa." I told him that one of my dreams was to give the kids everything I never had growing up. He looked at me with a smile on his face and asked, "why? You didn't have everything growing up, and look how you turned out." That conversation changed my perspective on how I would raise my children; that I didn't need to give them everything, I just needed to give them enough.

Question: Have you ever said to yourself, "I want my child to be better than when I was growing up." Did you start to reflect on the things you didn't want them to experience that you experienced? How did you eliminate those scenarios or teach them to respond differently than you did when you were younger?

Life lessons are meant to be understood and passed on through advice, conversations, and stories you can look back on and laugh all while teaching. This is how our children become better than we were at their age.

Never Let Them See You Sweat

One of the worst things to see is your child hurting. I remember when KJ was about 4 years old and we were having a "staycation" at one of the hotels in Las Vegas. Jaelin, my niece Jada, and KJ were watching a movie in the other room and all of a sudden, I heard screaming. I jumped up and ran to the other room. All I saw was KJ crying in his sleep, but he was also convulsing. I tried waking him, but he would not wake up. Tasha started crying and asking the kids what happened. At that time I just picked him up and started saying, "Hey buddy, dad is here. It's okay. You can stop crying." But he continued crying and wouldn't wake up, so Tasha called 911. By the time the paramedics got there, he had stopped crying and slowly opened his eyes. When they checked him, he was just fine. We took him to the hospital and found that he had had a seizure. A "Febrile Seizure" to be precise, which is common in healthy children according to the doctor, but it still freaked me out. I thought I was losing my son and I didn't know what to do except talk to him. I wasn't going to panic. When you panic, you can't think. So I stayed cool, and it paid off because everyone else also calmed down. The thing is, you never know who's watching you. If you're calm, they stay calm; if you're nervous, they will be nervous.

Well, that theory got tested several times because that was not the last time he would have a seizure. Each time I would just talk to him and though I was panicking on the inside, I stayed cool as a fan. My wife was panicking enough for the both of us and I knew it wouldn't help anyone to hear me panicking too. I never knew if he heard me, but the way his body responded as he calmed down gave me confirmation that staying calm and communicating with him no matter what helped. As the years passed, he would have fewer and fewer seizures, but we continued to communicate the same.

Question: Do you recall a time when you saw your parent(s) panic or upset, and you knew something was not right? How did it make you feel? Looking back, it may or may not have been something to panic about.

Having the ability to shield our children from the worries of the world through strength and confidence will show them how to approach tough situations in their lives.

Communication Is Key

In my opinion, communication is the key, but it has to be proper communication, delivered at the right time and in the right way. When KJ was in third grade, his teacher called us in for a meeting before school. Even though he was a good kid, he often spoke his mind. His teacher assured us that nothing was wrong but wanted to discuss something with us. When we met up with the teacher KJ, was standing with us. I asked him if he wanted to stay and listen to what we were talking about and he said no, so I let him go play with his friends. Whatever this teacher wanted to talk to us about did not make KJ nervous or give him any anxiety. Whatever he had done he felt justified and was not worried at all. The confidence he displayed said it all.

The teacher told us that KJ was sometimes a bit chatty in class and would leave his desk a lot, so she spoke sternly to him and told him to quiet down and go back to his seat. She said that after class, he came up to her and asked to speak with her privately. She agreed and said, "what's up?" She went on to tell us how KJ told her "not embarrass him in class and if she wants him to do something, all she needs to do is say, 'KJ, stay on task' and he would know that means, to stop messing around and get back to work." I told her I would speak to him, and she said, "no, I'm very impressed by how he delivered that message to me," and she wanted to let us know that he was a good kid overall. She just never expected a third grader to set her straight as he did. Most adults can't even do that.

Another example of my son's strength of communication, I recall happened when he was eleven years old. KJ could hold a conversation with anyone and would have confidence and clear delivery. From the barbershop to the board room, he made people stop and listen.

During one of the national "Take Your Kids to Work Days," KJ was with all of the other children doing different activities until one of the admins asked if I could come to see what the children were doing. I followed her to the training room, peeked in, and there he was, standing at the podium while all of the other children were sitting there listening intently. I asked her what was going on and she said, "he told everyone to sit down because he was going to train them." I was so proud! At the time, I had been promoted to Initial Sales Trainer and I would share with him what I did at work every day. You see, communication is as much about listening as it is talking, and he was clearly good at both.

At my brother-in-law's barbershop, he would have conversations with everyone from the youngsters to the elders. From hip-hop to politics to sports and then flip to black history. He was in every conversation. I think some of the fellas came to the shop just to have conversations with him. It was exciting to watch him communicate with everyone in the shop while all the kids his age sat back and watched in awe. I don't know if it was how we communicated with him as a baby or not, but it was like nothing I had ever seen before.

It all starts with the CONNECTION

I tell you these stories to say, the most important thing you can give your child is the connection to you and the freedom to communicate on their terms. They will only get that if you give it to them. The connection to express with no judgment is liberating in adults. Can you imagine if you gave your child the confidence to speak up or stand up for what they believe in? The connection to feel protected even when they know they did wrong or feel ashamed? It gives them the self-confidence we all want to instill in our children.

On my fiftieth birthday, my seventeen-year-old son sent me a text. In that text, he told me that "I was his hero and though I may be known for inspiring people with my quote GET UP, I love you son, is what inspires him the most." It brought tears to my eyes just reading it. See, for young people, it's hard to express themselves, especially for boys. Create that connection now so they feel comfortable enough to express themselves and live life on their terms as they get older.

THE MESSAGE: You may not be sure what to do; do it anyway and watch. You might not know what to say; say it anyway, and then listen to the response. We are not perfect, but remember to give them the best part of you and let them do the rest. You are the living example that they see daily. You are the foundation for everything they will become. It all has to start with communication. The days of "because I said so" are gone. Open the door to the best part of you, so your child can be the best version of themselves.

There was never any "baby talk." No goo, gaa gaa, and no pacifiers with our children. So, when we had those crying moments (and we had those A LOT!), we would pick up our babies and talk to them. In those moments of emergency, we didn't panic, we communicated. Communication was very important to us and though our babies couldn't talk, they could understand what we were saying or the emotion we used. To this day I still tell my twenty-five-year-old daughter and seventeen-year-old son I love them. They need to hear it just as much as I need to say it.

Parents: I implore you, create that "Family Connection." If you don't, the internet will be your child's family connection. The streets will be your child's family connection. The lessons you are teaching through your action will play a pivotal role for generations to come. So, spend the time talking to your children, but make sure you listen to their thoughts and perspectives because Time Is Life and you just don't know how much time you have left. Break the cycle of "cause I said so!" with "Do you understand why?" This creates communication. Lastly, believe in your teachings and trust that the "Family Connection" is strong.

Stacia Gowens et al.

INTRODUCING P. QUAKE PLETCHER

P. Quake Pletcher has been a son to many, was a husband for a period, and is a father to two daughters. The P stands for Perspicacious, but due to inaccurate branding, hides this behind the initial. Quake had the blessing and curse of growing up a Hoosier, but had the good fortune of living on the South and the West Coasts, as well as Asia and Africa, to round out his understanding of the world. Quake had the good sense to get a B.A. from Indiana University and an M.B.A. where the spoiled children roam in Southern California. Quake has familiarized himself with failures and falls as an entrepreneur and hiking around the world. At one point, he could order a beer if he pleased in nineteen different languages and fight taxi drivers in four of those.

A career that reflects nothing so much as a long nap spoiled, he has found him counting beans for propeller heads, stocking shelves at big box retailers, and trying to find cures for cancers, or at least some respite from their ravages. But these days he mainly shows up at the wrong door to pick up a kid or offers himself up to be mocked while filmed dancing the latest jig by a daughter for her TakkyTok™ page. Such are the consequences of returning to your home state to spawn and die. Given the nutty politics of a state that elected Pence as governor, he is resolved, as Daniel Kaluuya was when he ran up into that crazy mess of white folk in the country, to Get Out of the Hoosier state and Blaxit to warmer climes to bake until well done (or die).

LEARNING TO FALL, UP

As a guy walking this earth, I am not much for roles or reverence. It's something that gives me more than a little bit of pause. Am I doing right by my daughters by not preparing them for social norms and expectations? So far, they have a low tolerance for suffering through discomfort and indignities, whether it be the clothes they wear or low-key encounters with the "-isms" they face. I imagine time will reveal the costs and/or benefits of such an approach to parenting. I simply love that my daughters are being raised with degrees of freedom from which to navigate their identity largely unheard of in human history. And they seem prepared to explore all of it, even while shouldering a fair amount of anxiety.

Free to Be: A Guiding Principle

When I started on this journey as a daddy, I can't say I ever gave the role much conscious thought. I mean, I wanted to be good at it. When someone hands me the ball, I really get focused. One, don't turn it over. Two, try to get a bucket. My first move was diving into those *Idiots with a Baby* books. I was not gonna be fumbling this baby. She is getting swaddled and powdered and fed according to best practices and standards. None of it was natural except the effort. But that first summer I made a choice that was not exactly conscious. I mean, I *really* never imagined myself as a dad. I live in the moment pretty well, so maybe noodling over how to parent isn't to be expected without the actual child present. But that first summer and for summers stretching out almost for the first decade after the crown princess arrived, I settled into the hammock with a book that seemed natural to me. And with my baby girl in one arm, I read aloud about Atticus and Scout and

Jem and Calpurnia and sadly, Tom. I felt that fatherhood blueprint in *To Kill A Mockingbird* in my marrow.

Let these children be free. Let them roam. Let them have just enough sense about social norms to not be cast out of the community, unless and until they give you a dang good reason to set yourself outside of it. And let them take up with verve and confidence things that may thrill or fulfill or simply leave a bit of bruising and wreckage. In that opening scene of the film version, this is captured in Scout's rolling inside the tire out of control and crashing into the dreaded house of Boo Radley.

So I don't know how much the girls got out of those swinging story sessions inside the screened-in porch with lightning bugs and lawnmowers in the background. But for me, I think it helped me push the girls sometimes a bit uncomfortably into spaces that were a little risky.

The Crown Princess: Emma Lucille

The crown princess, she was always a little more cautious. But she got nudged into snake handling and cliff jumping, among other things. Of course, there was the time at horseback riding where her little sister, the Usurper Princess, ran at the riding ring with an umbrella, making the horse skittish and then bolt. The CP had the presence of mind to yank back on the reins. However, she was not well versed in physics. As the horse came to an abrupt stop, the CP flew "ass over teakettle" and landed in the muddy ring. Minutes later, she was back on the thousand-pound stallion and in control. At seven years old. She went on to be a violence-embracing inner-tuber. Screaming behind the boat, she demanded faster whipping and bigger waves, some at the same time, to see just how she would smash and fly and stay on. She handled it with as much skill and courage as a PBA champion bull rider.

The Usurper Princess: Ella Winsome

But it was the Usurper Princess who truly embraced these lessons. She was an early acolyte. One day after a hard rain, we went in search of natural slides in the state park. This consisted of finding steep hills and just sitting and sliding. After the CP led, the UP…all of three years old, ran down the steep incline. This was actually more like base jumping (where folk jump off of bridges, skyscrapers, and mountainsides with a parachute). Except she had no chute. But after crashing in a pile of leaves at the bottom, she rose all smiles and just wanted to see the video.

After learning to ride her bike, she quickly earned the nickname "Crashella," with regular spills into the grass (as taught) or concrete (if inevitable) that she shook off. And then there was the tree climbing. One evening while she was up a tree, I heard a loud crack. I spun to see Crashella free falling between the branches before snagging the last branch with her right hand. I rushed over to have her drop into my arms, but she waved me off and plunged the last bit into the bed of pine needles below.

Our dog, Calpurnia Scout, was a German-engineered hunting dog. She was built for performance and one way to unleash it was to tie her up to the sled when it snowed. Ella assumed the position of Musher after an early snowfall, and Callie took off down the slight, graded parking lot near the boat docks. Callie gained speed and I realized she was going to do what her instincts told her, which was to go out on the docks and launch herself into the icy water to retrieve a fowl (or ball). Ella screamed with innocent delight as they accelerated toward the water. In horror, I screamed at her to "rollover, rollover!" and to her credit, she did a decent stop-drop-and-roll at maximum velocity. With laughter and snow covering her melanated rosy-bronze cheeks, I sighed at the near miss.

Adventures in Finding Our Own Level

Before long, we found ourselves at Seneca Rocks, West Virginia on Fall Break. We had the mountain to ourselves because it's better to be lucky than good and we showed up on a beautiful autumn day when the rest of the climbing community had gone South since the season was over. Our guide set us up at Humphrey's Head and I went first, getting about 20 feet up before my weight and my muscle maxed out. Then the CP went and got about 40 feet up the face of the cliff before tapping out. Finally, the UP started, and before long was 60 feet above us. Then the tears started, and fatherly words of encouragement were met with the venom of a seriously irritated seven-year-old. It's an interesting position to be in when your baby girl is 40 feet above your ability to help, on the side of a mountain, and tears are raining down as you stare up from your base ledge, helpless. By interesting, I think I mean terrifyingly impotent. Then she lost her grip and fell, as the guide leaned back and the rope went taut. But the little honey badger regained her footing and gritted out a climb that didn't stop until she was standing on the peak of Humphrey's Head, 80 feet above us and thousands of feet above the valley. There, she had a view I wistfully realized I will never see. (I should have put a GoPro on her helmet).

But there I was, helpless to help. And with some skill at falling and spit and grit, the UP rose until she could rise no more. And there is simply no way I will ever be in her shoes. She rose above me. What more could a father ask for his child? These children, I helped learn to fall. But now they rise up.

Present Fatherhood

Reflecting on my parenting journey, I've heard more than a few times that the best thing about my parenting is that I am present, and I haven't always received that well. Believe me, it can still chafe at me to hear it. Presence seems the lowest bar for fatherhood. But even if you take it at face value, where one shows up consistently for birthdays and dance recitals and games, I think that is worthy. I've seen too many children light up and do better with this basic presence. But I also encourage expanded presence. It's the presence that thinks hard about the question to ask your sons and daughters and the mindfulness to listen to the answer and respond accordingly, validating the child. And in my own particular case, I think extending presence into riskier spaces has meant that I am deeply in tune with where they are with spidey senses activated in case I need to leap in to support them. Often that means acting like I am not paying attention, while the girls navigate their challenges with focused independence. But watching these girls fall and rise is my reward, and if I wasn't indeed "present" in those moments, I would miss one of the most satisfying privileges of being their father.

And as they grow into their tween and teen years, I see that independence in how they navigate the stresses of social injustice and a devastating pandemic. I see how they evolve their identity and challenge me to think in ways conventional society did not prepare me for. It's liberating as a father to not try to superimpose traditional mindsets but to center their health and happiness. This is the highest form presence takes for me personally and provides the biggest blessings.

So, I have 4 things a dad can ask themselves to be a Present Father.

1. What event is going on that is the most important thing in my child's world today, this week, this month and how am I going to be there? *(Watch them present)*
2. What am I going to ask my child to understand how they are experiencing the world and what is important to them? *(Present their ideas, emotions back to them)*
3. How can I position my child to be stretched but present enough to catch them when they fall or lift them up after they land? *(Be present for safety/security)*
4. When my child makes choices about where to be, what to wear, who to like/love, what interests to pursue, can I support it because it promotes his/her/their health and happiness rather than force convention/tradition that may be unhealthy and create unhappiness? *(Give the present of affirming love)*

INTRODUCING ROBERT HURD, SR.

Robert Hurd, Sr. is a father and husband, married to Diane McMillan-Hurd for twenty-two years. He was born in Jackson, Michigan in 1950 to an unmarried teen mother. He has lived in Grand Rapids, Michigan for roughly fifty years.

THE HONOR OF BEING A BONUS DAD

The Early Years

Some people in America are born with the right zip code, giving them health, wealth, and the opportunity for a bright future. Unfortunately, this was not the case for me. I was born to a teen mother who lived with her parents in the poorest area of Jackson, Michigan. Because of the limited career options in that small town during the 1950s, my mother decided to move 70 miles east to Detroit, Michigan, and I was left in Jackson with my maternal grandparents, who cared for me until their passing in the Spring of 1967 and Spring 1968.

The Fatherhood Challenge

Fatherhood, like many other roles in life, is full of challenges. Fathers aren't born knowing how to effectively be a father and soon realize how difficult it is to be something you have never seen up close. Our cars come with an owner's manual, giving us step-by-step instructions on how to get the best performance out of the vehicle. That's not so with children who, after birth, are placed in your arms with little or no instructions on how to care for your infant. It's sink or swim once you walk out of the hospital doors. So many of life's challenges come with the opportunity to get a "do-over" if you mess it up the first time. Out of the myriad of choices we make on our incredible journey from the cradle to the grave, no experience equals the importance of parenthood. I quickly learned there are no do-overs, only "do-betters!"

As our children enter this world, we view their futures with great optimism, believing that they can and will achieve remarkable success. Yet, at the same time, looking back at my life, I remember when I fell prey to some of life's pitfalls that awaited me in each decade.

My First Fatherhood Role Model

The father's role in the growth and development of his children is of immense importance. Fathers serve many critical functions, including progenitor, provider, protector, adviser, and confidante. My biological father served as my progenitor and provided me with my first name, and that was it. Unfortunately, he drowned in a fishing accident in 1954. Although I had no brothers or sisters, I was blessed to have nine aunts and uncles and my maternal grandfather and grandmother.

So, my first fatherhood model was my mother's father, Clinton Hurd, born in 1896. He was an old World War I veteran and a stern disciplinarian who taught me how to behave and how to work. I got no hugs, no lap time, and no words of encouragement. I did have second-hand clothes, a roof over my head, and daily meals. I felt abandoned by my mother and unloved. As I considered the other 80 percent of the kids in my neighborhood who were living with both parents, I wondered, "Why not me?" Birthdays and Christmas would come, and I didn't receive a single present!

Life is very hard without a father around, and it's even tougher without a mother. So, at eleven years old, I began to think that if things were going to get any better in life, I needed to change my approach.

Get to Work!

My pre-adolescent and teen years were a time of growth and development. I began to understand that I needed resources for living that no one else would provide. So, I started to ask myself, "What skills do I have that will allow me to legally make money?" Many fathers in the neighborhood were fishermen, so I checked the prices at the local bait shops, and I sold crickets and nightcrawlers (worms) at a 50 percent discount. I also got my grandfather's rake and snow shovel and walked around the neighborhood, knocking on doors offering my services for raking leaves in the fall and shoveling snow in the winter for a fee. These gigs gave me funds between eleven and fourteen years old to get haircuts and buy shoes and school clothes.

A Teen's View of Manhood

I thought I was pretty cool when I was fifteen years old because I had excellent haircuts and clothes from Detroit. My view of manhood at fifteen was:

1) Being able to handle yourself in a fight.

2) Hanging out with teen friends experimenting with alcohol and drugs.

3) Having girlfriends. If one girlfriend was good, many must be better!

I attended a large high school of about 4,000 students, where about 20 percent of the students were Black. In the first marking period of my sophomore year, I was passing only my gym class with a D grade. At the beginning of my sophomore year, I failed all my other courses and ended up with a .25 grade point average. I had three teachers (out of the forty-five teachers I had from kindergarten to high school graduation) who gave me words of encouragement. These teachers said, "This work is not too hard for you! Try harder!" So, I did, and my grades improved to A's, B's, and sometimes a C. The other 4forty-two teachers treated me as though I was invisible.

College and Beyond: 20-29 Years Old

I started Jackson Community College (JCC) with hopes of transferring to a major university and pursuing a pre-medical curriculum. No one mentioned to me that Preparation + Opportunity = Success. My failure to take a college-prep curriculum in high school put me far behind my college counterparts on the pre-med track. Although I had As, Bs, and Cs, medical schools wanted 4.0 students. I wasn't getting it done. After much thought, I changed my major to education. I had to leave the university with a marketable degree! I also had a growth spurt from high school to community college, growing from around 5'10" to 6'8" at the end of my first year at JCC. I played basketball during my years at JCC, my first-time playing varsity sports at any level.

After getting my associate degree, I transferred to Grand Valley State University (GVSU) to pursue my education and play basketball. At the time, GVSU had an enrollment of about 10 percent African American students, of which I estimate 20 percent were serious about their education. The rest of the students were in college to have a good time and not about getting a degree. I spent many hours in the college library, and I observed that I was the only athlete there. When I graduated from GVSU, I was named a Top Ten Graduate as a diverse representation of how the college impacted the community.

I wasn't having much luck finding a teaching job after graduation. A business professor helped me by recommending me for a low-level white-collar job at the Kalamazoo General Motors Plant. I worked there for two years and received enough compensation to pay for my master's degree in counseling from Western Michigan University. After that, I worked at Kalamazoo Valley Community College (KVCC) as a tutorial specialist in their Learning Lab. After I finished my degree, I was promoted to Assistant Director of Admissions at KVCC.

My First Marriage

I figured I was grown up at age twenty-six After all, I had matured since my teen years, and I viewed my life as if I could handle anything. After high school, I successfully obtained my associate's, bachelor's, and master's degrees. Most of my friends were getting married or having kids out of wedlock, so I thought that a wife and kids were the next steps on my life journey. I found a nice girl who was both beautiful and intelligent, so we dated for about a year, and then I asked her to marry me. As 20-somethings, we had a fairy tale view of marriage as all good and happy times. I never considered that you and/or your spouse may have some bad days, and heaven help you if it is the *same* day. Even if you are not the cause of those bad days, you may still end up paying the price. Many young couples don't consider that you must work continuously to grow together instead of forming differing world views and growing apart. This takes intentionality, patience, prayer, and time.

With our three active kids at home, my wife needed a break, so she wanted to sleep in on the weekends. So, I took over as the cook for the kids and was on cartoon duty. I later realized that neither of us felt appreciated by the other. My practice of hanging out with the fellows angered my wife, so she cut back on intimacy. As a spoiled, former athlete in my college days, I was faithful to my wife in the first years of our marriage. But finding myself with unmet physical needs, I gave in to a few of the constant offers from women that came my way even though I was married. I played that dangerous game. This was an unforgivable mistake as far as my wife was concerned. When she mentioned getting a divorce, I said, "Fine!" I grabbed a few things and left. In hindsight, we should have given each other more time to consider how divorcing would affect all five of us. I forgave her years ago, but she never forgave me, and I have to live with that burden.

After my first wife, Denise and I divorced in the late 1980s, she moved with my children to Washington, D.C. to be closer to her family. I felt I was Villain #1, persona non grata, an outlaw; but I was determined to be a presence in my children's lives.

My Children

Our first daughter, Dana, came in the mid-1970s, and she was cute, intelligent, and energetic. She was reading three-syllable words at 2 ½ years old, so we started her in the first grade at 4 years old. We were proud and happy with her placement, but many of her classmates were jealous and started picking on her. So, I taught her how to make a fist and showed her where to punch. After my divorce from Denise, Dana stayed behind to live with me as she finished her senior year in high school and prepared to enroll at Iowa State University. Dana is an actress, following in her mother Denise's footsteps and she has starred in several roles with local acting companies. She is also a creative movie theater makeup artist and uses her gifts to make up wedding parties and even television personalities in the Baltimore/Washington, D.C. area.

Our family expanded in 1980 when our fraternal twins, Leslie and Bobby, were born. My son was born with special needs and was diagnosed with ADHD early on, and later with Asperger's Syndrome (Autism) with epilepsy. After Denise passed away in 2004, Bobby came to live with me and my current wife, Diane. Bobby is high functioning on the Asperger's scale, so we got him social security assistance and other resources, including job placement. Like me, Bobby has a strong work ethic and never missed a day in his four years of employment. Unfortunately, he was laid off at the start of the COVID-19 pandemic, so now I am helping him turn the page and start a new chapter in his life. Our daughter Leslie lived with us for about two years, working alongside me at a charter school in Muskegon, Michigan after the divorce. Leslie is a compassionate, ingenious, beautiful, and vivacious young woman who teaches pre-school in Washington, D.C., working on her master's degree in pre-school education.

The Second Marriage: Enter the Bonus Daughters

I remember the first time I saw Diane. It was at the Michigan State University Kellogg Conference Center. The event was the MSU Conference on the Survival of the Black Male. I was the Director of the Grand Rapids Community College Upward Bound program and the adviser for GRCC's Black Student Union. As the assistant principal at Lansing Everett High School, Diane was the chaperone for a couple of dozen black male students. I was struck by her commitment, poise, and beauty.

A few years later, I was the DJ at an event that Diane and a few of her sorority sisters attended. After the event, I called out to the group as they were leaving and asked them where the after-party was. They mentioned a hangout spot, and I told them I would meet them after dropping off my equipment at my house. (Diane told me years later that she didn't think I would show up.) I got home, unloaded my stuff, took a shower, and hurried off to the spot. When I got there, it was a little later than I expected, and it looked like Diane and her friends were getting ready to leave, so I approached her table and asked her to dance to a song called *Whip Appeal*. At the end of the dance, it seemed like she was as interested in me as I was in her.

Bonus Daughter #1: Stacia

The first time I entered Diane's home, I was greeted by her high school senior daughter and three of her posse standing behind her. Bonus daughter #1, who is about 14 inches shorter than me, stepped up boldly and said, "What are your intentions as it pertains to my mother?" I was surprised by her bold and direct approach, but I was elated that she and her crew were 100 percent Team Lady Diane. Stacia is a typical McMillan woman: Strong, outspoken, intelligent, ambitious, confident, and of course, beautiful. She is Head of Marketing, Client Experience at AMN Healthcare. Her former work experiences include Marketing Consultant at Galderma, Vice President of Global Marketing Services at SomnoMed North America, and Marketing Manager at Eli Lilly and Company. I am and will always be 100 percent in her corner.

Bonus Daughter #2: Shannon

When I started dating Diane, Shannon was about eight years old. At the end of one particular visit, as I was preparing to leave for Grand Rapids, Shannon came up and gave me the biggest hug. This worried me because I never want to hurt children emotionally. I feel that adults are tough and resilient, allowing them to bounce back from hurt and disappointment. But not kids, who I view as more fragile. I stopped calling Diane at that point, and we lost touch for about eight years.

Lucky for me, Diane kept bringing me up in conversations with one of her best friends. One day her friend had enough and told her, "Just call him! At least you will know where you stand!" Diane called me at work while I was outside loading students on the buses. Remember, Diane was an assistant principal in Lansing, so she figured that I would be supervising bus dismissal. She told me a few years later that she hightailed it out of her office to go to her bus duty. Diane said she wanted to leave a message—she was a little nervous about hearing my voice after so many years. She wanted me to call her back. I guess she thought that if I didn't call her back, that would be a sign that our romance was truly over, and she would move on. I called her back as soon as I saw her message, and we have been together ever since.

I was blessed to see Shannon graduate from JW Sexton High School. I drove her down to Tallahassee a few times to help her move into her Florida A&M University student apartment. During Parent Day, we visited her classes and experienced several HBCU homecomings and her college graduation. She received her bachelor of science degree and her master of business administration degree on the same day from the acclaimed FAMU School of Business Institute (SBI). Shannon's specialty is Organizational Change, a much-needed training niche, in the Human Relations Department of Boehringer Ingelheim Pharmaceuticals. She has worked for Accenture, Deloitte, McKesson, Coca-Cola, and Boehringer Ingelheim Pharmaceuticals. Shannon is a woman of faith, loyal, intelligent, musically gifted, beautiful, and sensitive. She knows I will always be there to support her in her major decisions in life.

Becoming Grandpa Bob

My two grandchildren are a significant part of my life. It has been a great joy watching them grow into outstanding young adults. Chris is studious, patient, kind, and loving. He mastered his mechanical engineering curriculum at Prairie View A&M University, and he now works for General Dynamics Electric Boat in Groton, Connecticut.

Alexa has the characteristics of a long line of McMillan women, including strong-willed, intelligent, beautiful, and, of course, outspoken. Their parents sent Chris and Alexa to spend four or five weeks with Diane and me in the summer. Our grandchildren had amazing vacations and were a ton of fun for us as grandparents. These vacations also allowed their parents to have some couple time.

I got to be actively involved in our grandchildren's lives by attending their sports teams from their pee-wee leagues through varsity sports. We also watched them navigate their way from elementary school through college, which has been exciting and rewarding. As they transition to adulthood, I am incredibly proud of their adult versions and know that the best is yet to come. I love them both with all my heart.

The Amazing Dr. Joe Mac: My Second Fatherhood Role Model

My father-in-law, Dr. Joseph McMillan, Sr., was a magnificent man. He was well-read, outspoken, passionate, committed, faithful, and fearless. His dedication to the growth and development of the Black community was without question. He often explained, "I am not against anybody; I'm just **FOR** my people!" His leadership was evident in the church community, K-12 education, the higher ed community, and local, state, and national political communities.

Dr. Mac, as he was affectionately known, worked on every level on behalf of families, young children, and students from pre-K through the doctorate levels. He was always a champion for the greater good of the Black community. Dr. Mac accepted me with open arms into his family and honored me by allowing me to take his only daughter's hand in marriage.

As a child of the 1960s, I watched the awakening of cultural pride in Black America. As a child, to be called "Black" by someone was a huge putdown. They were fighting words. But by the late 1960s, we were singing, "Say it loud! I'm Black, and I'm proud!" The first adult male family member I could talk to about the struggle was Dr. Joseph McMillan. He was the convener of the University of Louisville National Black Family Conference for over thirty years. This conference gathered community leaders, social workers, educators, parents, activists, students, as well as anyone who believed in equal opportunities for all people. Dr. Mac gathered the top thought leaders of Black America to discuss the many important issues of the day. He was and still is revered as an elder by activists and students from across this nation. I am forever grateful that I had the opportunity to gain wisdom from this Giant of Giants and call him "Papa."

What is a Bonus Dad?

A stepfather is a man married to your mother. This term carries no special significance, other than this is the next man your mother chooses to marry. A Bonus Dad is a man who has entered not just your mother's life but also that of the children as an added bonus. It's almost as if the children have hit the Lotto when it comes not only to mom's happiness, but also to additional support and love in their own lives.

When my two Bonus Daughters started calling me their Bonus Dad, I was filled with joy that they welcomed my input, not only in the life of their mother but also in their lives as well. I have enthusiastically stepped up to make myself available to assist them in any way I can.

Beware of Fool's Gold

Many of the men who shared their experiences in this book were dealt a tough hand to play in the game of life. They ventured out into the world without an experienced guide to share their experiences and learn from their mistakes. Yet, as long as fathers are alive, they serve in critical, essential roles. They are our providers, protectors, and life coaches for our children. I hope that my recollections provide insights into the nurturance options we have as fathers.

In the 1800s, to entice young men to go West, many stories were circulated in America east of the Mississippi that these youth should go West in search of gold for fame and fortune. In their Westward exploration, many found iron pyrite, also known as Fool's Gold. The phrase Fool's Gold is a way to describe something that, despite its appearance, is not valuable or authentic. This world is full of shiny things that are worthless in the grand scheme of things, like cars, clothes, fame, power, and some beautiful women. Each of us is challenged daily to pursue those things that we value. What do you believe in? What's worth living for? What's worth dying for?

Fatherhood is the most critical role a man can play. This role is not a single destination but rather a lifelong journey that continues through the decades of our lives. In each decade, we pick up more clues on how to do this fatherhood thing right. To become strong fathers, we must constantly search for best practices for raising our progeny. In seeking out what works with one child, we may need other options for our next child. We quickly learn no two children are alike.

I have offered you a view of my life experiences so that you can anticipate some potential pitfalls and weigh your possible options. Of course, no father is perfect, but we surely will be alright if we approach every member of our household and our family with compassion, love, and respect.

Stacia Gowens et al.

ABOUT THE COORDINATOR

STACIA GOWENS

S tacia A. Gowens is the visionary behind *Tales from Fatherhood*. She recognized the fathers in her life could serve as strong role models for all fathers; those new to the Dad role, to those who now have the honor of being a Grandfather and every father in between. Stacia is a born Spartan (Go Green) and was raised in Lansing, MI. She holds a Bachelor of Arts and a Master of Business Administration both from Michigan State University. She is married to the love of her life, Edward Gowens, who is one of this work's featured authors. They have two amazing children, Christopher and Alexa.

Made in the USA
Middletown, DE
25 May 2022

66110253R00097